Successful Salesforce Projects 101

Successful Salesforce Projects 101

The Client's Guide to Stress-Free Implementation

By Pei Mun Lim

Successful Salesforce Projects 101
The Client's Guide to Stress-Free Implementation

Copyright © 2024 Pei Mun Lim

ISBN: 9798345801130
Imprint: Independently published

All rights reserved. No part of this book may be reproduced or transmitted in any form or by any means, electronic or mechanical, including photocopying, recording or by any information storage and retrieval system without permission from the author. For permissions contact: info@zenhaotraining.co.uk.

Every effort has been taken in the preparation of this book. However, the author and publisher assumes no responsibilities for errors or omissions, or damages that may result from the use of information contained in this book.

What Readers are saying

"Pei shares her 30+ years leading enterprise CRM implementations and beautifully crafted into an end-to-end CRM implementation resource that any project manager just starting their career must read! Bakes in humor, data, and real-world scenarios, along with an appendix filled with resources to help you ace your next Salesforce project implementation.
10/10 recommend."

- Tristan Lombard, Stage Mom

The guidebook every project team needs to reduce risk and ensure a successful outcome! As per usual, Pei breaks it down with empathy and perspective to illustrate what's important and why, including recognition of the the needs and motivations of the humans involved. Your boss will thank you, so grab your copy today!

- Jodi Hrbek, Author of Rock your Role as a Salesforce Admin

"I absolutely looooooooved your book! You bring the human element of project management to life, combining Agile principles with heartfelt storytelling that makes each lesson relatable and memorable. The quote "Build a bridge of trust so strong it can bear the weight of truth" is one I'll carry with me—thank you for creating such an inspiring guide!"

- Erica Kelly, Business Analyst & Project Manager

Rarely do you come across experts with battle scars to prove their vast experience who are also able to explain concepts so clearly that even a 4-year-old can understand them! Thankfully, Pei is now sharing her wisdom for all of us to benefit. Successful Salesforce Projects 101 covers everything from project business case to go-live and beyond. Through humor and practical, realistic examples, she demonstrates how to navigate the often high-stress project conversations effectively. If you're a client-side project manager or executive, this is the book you've been waiting for to get superpowers and donuts to shepherd your Salesforce project safely to harbor.

- Kristian Margaryan Jørgensen, Author of Salesforce End-to-End Implementation Handbook and Founder of GoElephant

"Pei's new book is a valuable resource for anyone involved in Salesforce implementation projects. Pei's book offers a thorough and practical approach to the entire implementation lifecycle, from initial planning to post-deployment support. It's an easy and fun read complete with adorable doodles to illustrate her points. I definitely recommend it and will be adding it to my Salesforce toolbox!"

- Gabie Caballero, Lead Salesforce Enablement Program Manager

"This new book has #OnThePeiroll magic throughout. It's instantly infectious in that it's easy to follow and honest in its approach. It draws you in through Pei's knowledge and words of wisdom from her many years of experience in the consulting world."

- Ben Duong, freelance Salesforce marketing consultant

"There's possibly no one better than Pei Mun Lim to guide you through the journey delivering a great Salesforce implementation. Here she shares the benefit of her humanity, calmness, and ability to listen to produce a holistic guide to sustainable Salesforce solutions. You want fewer headaches - there's always some as Pei points out with her honest approach - and a happier workplace? You got it!"

- Paul Ginsberg, Salesforce Golden Hoodie and ADHD Coach

"Successful Salesforce Project 101 is the perfect guidebook for any team looking to implement Salesforce. This book breaks down the crucial steps that can make all the difference in the success of your CRM projects in a fun and easy-to-understand way. Whether your company is thinking about levelling up your CRM practices or you work with clients on Salesforce projects, this book will deepen your understanding of the end-to-end Salesforce implementation process—taking you from initial planning and building a business case to successful go-live and beyond!"

- Amy Morris, Salesforce Consultant

Table of content

THE BUSINESS CASE 1

1 RECOGNISING THE NEED FOR CHANGE 2
    Organisational self-awareness 5
    Conduct thorough internal assessments 5
    Gather Comprehensive Feedback 5
    Foster a Culture of Open Communication 7

2 CRAFTING A COMPELLING BUSINESS CASE 9
    The Analysis 14
    The Power of Clear Objectives 15
    Quantify Potential Benefits (ROI and Efficiency Gains) 15
    Address risks and mitigation strategies 16

3 SECURING EXECUTIVE BUY-IN 18
    Delivering a Compelling Presentation 22
    Tailor your presentation to your audience 22
    Use data to support your arguments 23
    Anticipate and address potential objections 24

4 PREPARING THE REQUEST FOR PROPOSAL (RFP) 26
    Crafting an Effective RFP 30
    Engaging Key Stakeholders 30
    Include evaluation criteria in the RFP 31
    Get the legal team to review RFP 31

DISCOVERY & PLANNING 33

5 PREPARING FOR PARTNER ENGAGEMENT 34
    Setting Up Partner Engagement for Success 38
    Establishing a Governance Framework 38
    Planning for Change Management and Communication 39
    Preparing the Internal Team for Partner Collaboration 40

6 ANALYSIS AND REQUIREMENTS GATHERING 42
    Business Analysis and Requirements Specification 47
    Current and Future State Process Analysis 47
    Defining Clear Scope and Requirements 48
    Data Cleansing and Migration Planning 48

7 DESIGN & PLANNING 50
    Design and Planning for Project Success 54
    Making Design Decisions 54
    Defining Success Metrics and KPIs 55
    Risk Assessment and Mitigation Planning 55

8 RESOURCING, FINANCING & PARTNERSHIPS 57
    Capacity Building, Capital and Collaborations 61
    Resourcing the Project Team 61
    Budget Planning and Cost Management.. 62
    Partner Management and Collaboration Strategies 63

9 EVALUATING DELIVERABLES AND VENDOR PROPOSALS 64
    The Beauty Pageant: Evaluating Vendor Proposals........................... 68
    Evaluating Discovery Deliverables.. 68
    Use a Standardised Scoring System 69
    Consider Cultural Fit and Technical Capabilities 69

10 FROM DISCOVERY TO IMPLEMENTATION 71
    Transitioning From Discovery to Implementation 74
    Knowledge Transfer and Team Continuity 74
    Internal Readiness and Stakeholder Alignment 74
    Project Scope and Readiness Checklist 75

PROJECT IMPLEMENTATION 77

11 THE BUILD PART OF THE PROJECT 78
    Client Involvement in the CRM Build Phase 83
    Consistent and Timely Communication 83
    Meaningful and Actionable Feedback... 83
    Align Implementation with Business Objectives 84

12 PLANNING FOR QUALITY.. 86
    Planning for User Acceptance Testing... 89
    Select and Train the Right UAT Team.. 89
    Develop a Comprehensive Test Plan 90
    Prepare Realistic Test Data 90

13 USER ACCEPTANCE TESTING (UAT) 92
    User Acceptance Testing in CRM Implementation............................ 96
    Defects and Change Requests 96
    Robust Issue Logging and Triage Processes 97
    Ensure a Smooth and Efficient UAT Process 97

14 CHANGE MANAGEMENT & USER ADOPTION 99
    Skills Development and User Engagement...................................... 102
    Craft a Compelling Change Narrative 102
    Adopt an Experiential Learning Approach....................................... 102
    Generate Momentum with Early Wins and Celebration 103

15 GO-LIVE PREPARATION AND EXECUTION.. 105
    CRM Launch Readiness and Deployment.. 108
    The Comprehensive Go-Live Plan and Checklist 108
    Stakeholder Communication and Expectation Management 109
    Readiness Checks and Final Preparations 109

AFTER GO-LIVE **111**

16 HYPERCARE AND STABILISATION 112
    Post-Go-Live Support and Capability Building 116
    Hypercare Issue Resolution and Prioritisation Processes 116
    Monitoring of System Performance and User Adoption 116
    Knowledge Transfer and Building Internal Support Capability 117

17 PLANNING FOR CONTINUOUS IMPROVEMENT 119
    Key Practices for Ongoing Success 123
    The Feedback and Enhancement Process 123
    Regular System Health Checks 124
    Ongoing Training and Skill Development 124

A FINAL WORD FROM PEI **125**

APPENDIX **127**

SAMPLE BUSINESS CASE 128
    The Business Case for DataNova's Salesforce Implementation 128
    1. Executive Summary 128
    2. Business Need 128
    Problem Statement 129
    Strategic Alignment 129
    Current Situation Analysis 130
    3. Scope and Objectives 130
    Project Scope 130
    Objectives 131
    4. Options Analysis 132
    Option 1: In-House Implementation 132
    Option 2: External Salesforce Partner 133
    5. Cost-Benefit Analysis 134
    Costs 134
    Benefits 134
    ROI Calculation per year 135
    6. Risk Assessment 135
    7. Resource Requirements 136
    In-House Resources 136
    External Resources (if using partner) 136
    8. Implementation Timeline 137
    External Partner Timeline 137
    9. Stakeholder Analysis 138
    10. Recommendation 139
    11. Next Steps 139
    12. Appendices 140

Sample RFP 141
Request for Proposal (RFP) 141
CRM Implementation Discovery Phase for DataNova 141
1. Introduction 141
2. Company Background 141
3. Project Objectives 141
4. Scope of Work 141
5. Detailed CRM Requirements 142
6. Proposal Requirements 145
7. Evaluation Criteria 146
8. Submission Instructions 146
9. Questions and Clarifications 146
10. Selection Process 146
Sample Vendor Scoring Matrix 148
Glossary 152
Links & Resources 155
Connect with me 155
Podcasts & Articles I've done 156
Additional Resources & Articles 156

Acknowledgements

To my wonderful family—Jeff, my endlessly supportive ÜberHub and adventurous partner in life, Annabelle, Marcus, and Alex, my three amazing teenage ninja sprogs, and my ever-encouraging parents.

Thank you for being my foundation and my inspiration.

Superbig shoutout to my #StageMom Tristan Lombard whose unwavering faith and frequent gentle nudge helped me move forward with this book (and other things!) Love you so much!

Also my close friends and support circle who have carved out time to review this book: Caroline Häming, Eleanor Dearing, Nick Bryner, Justyna Krajewska, Caimin McGovern and Simon des Forges – thank you so much!

One more thing – I grew up learning the Queen's English, and therefore we aren't very partial to 'zees' in our spelling.

Organisation instead of organization.
Utilisation instead of utilization.

Sincere apologies to my American readers, so to make up for it, here are a few extra zees for you to use as you wish: z z z z zzzzz 😴

Also here's a lovely donut doodle from my youngest sprog.

Foreword

In 2020, when it seemed like everything we had taken for granted was collapsing in on itself, I sent a speculative message to Pei, looking for guidance on how improve my Salesforce consulting skills

in an effort to build some resilience in a career I loved, but seemed like it might vanish in a puff of smoke. I don't think I actually expected a reply, but not only did I get one - I got one which was not only open to helping but also genuinely optimistic about my prospects, providing just the encouragement I needed and exactly when I needed it most.

What started as a simple inquiry grew into an inspiring exchange of ideas about Salesforce adoption, implementation and best practice that's lasted 4 years and has even led me to be a guest on her podcast.

It's one thing to have the experience of multiple projects, but the great thing about Pei is that she's able to zoom out of that experience and identify themes, and so knows what to do and, probably more importantly, what not to do.

Pei and I typically work on opposite sides of the implementation cycle and so it's been really valuable to me to learn more about the decisions made early in the process and how small gaps can lead to bigger problems further down the line.

Through our conversations, I've been continually impressed by her depth of knowledge and her natural talent for explaining complex concepts with ease and that very specific sense of humour you're about to experience.

That same clarity, practicality and sense of fun shine through in this book. It's written with new Salesforce consultants in mind, but honestly, anyone in the consultancy field will walk away with fresh insights and actionable strategies.

Forget what you know about technical guides - this isn't one of them. It's much more than a guide; it's a conversation.

In her friendly, conversational tone, Pei brings to life real-world scenarios and provides concrete, actionable solutions.

She takes you through the challenges consultants like you will face every day, from managing client expectations to designing user-centred solutions, all in a way that feels like chatting with a trusted friend over coffee.

There are even passages that might make you laugh out loud—who says Salesforce consulting can't be fun?

I can say from experience that this is a book written by someone who truly understands the field and genuinely cares about helping others succeed.

I hope you'll find as much inspiration, knowledge, and enjoyment in these pages as I have!

Caimin McGovern
Salesforce Customer Success Director

Introduction

Welcome to "Successful Salesforce Projects 101: The Client's Guide to a Stress-Free Implementation"!

If you're holding this book, chances are you're about to embark on a Salesforce implementation journey, or you're curious about what it entails.

Either way, welcome!

I'm Pei Mun Lim, and I've been in the consulting world since I graduated many decades ago, in fact - for more years than I care to admit.

Throughout my career, I've implemented a few sexy CRM projects and have also seen some that have crashed and burned spectacularly (luckily not mine!).

This book is my attempt to share the lessons I've learned along the way, through scars I've accumulated or war stories from friends and colleagues who've managed to survive 'character-building' projects and come through the other side with sterling character to speak of!

What is the focus of this book?

This book focuses on the end-to-end lifecycle of implementing a new Customer Relationship Management (CRM) initiative, in this case – a new Salesforce instance from the client's perspective.

We'll walk through every stage of the journey, from recognising the need for a CRM to celebrating a successful go-live (and beyond).

But here's the twist – I'm not just going to throw a bunch of dry, technical jargon at you.

Instead, we'll follow the story of Uungu, a project manager at DataNova, a fictional company navigating their own Salesforce implementation.

Through their trials and triumphs, you'll learn practical strategies, avoid common pitfalls, and gain insights that you can apply to your own project.

Now, let's be clear about what this book isn't.

It's not a magical, one-size-fits-all manual that'll solve every Salesforce implementation challenge you might face.

Every company is unique, and so is every CRM project. This is not intended to be a rigid playbook with all the "right" answers.

Instead, think of this book as your friendly guide to the basics.

It aims to lay out the foundation and the building blocks of a successful Salesforce implementation.[1]

Think of it as using a solid pair of walking shoes and a compass to help guide you on your journey to your destination, instead of a detailed map of every possible route to get there.

Use the insights you gain here as a starting point.

Adapt them to your specific situation. Remember that while this book aims to help you ask the right questions, the final answers will always depend on your unique context.

Who is this book for?

This book is for anyone on the client side of a Salesforce implementation.

Whether you're a C-suite executive trying to understand the big picture, a project manager tasked with shepherding a beast of a project, or a team member who'll be using Salesforce day-to-day, there's something in here for you.

---

[1] While the word "Salesforce" appears multiple times in this book, the principles here can be applied to most software projects where an external implementation partner or vendor is involved.

You don't need to be a tech wizard to benefit from this book. In fact, if terms like 'API' and 'custom object' make you break out in a cold sweat, you're exactly who I had in mind when writing this.

My goal is to empower you with the knowledge to make informed decisions and effectively collaborate with your Salesforce implementation partner.[2]

This book is also for you if you are a collector of fine art. My pictorial elegance and mastery of expression has me likened to a modern day da Vinci.[3]

Who is this book **NOT** for?

This book isn't for those seeking deep technical dives into Salesforce configuration or custom development.

If you're looking for step-by-step guides on how to build complex formulas, intricate workflows, or custom Apex code, you might want to look elsewhere.

In fact, if you want a more detailed or advanced book on the topic, you should consider getting the **Salesforce End-to-End Implementation Handbook** written by my good friend, Kristian Margaryan Jørgensen.

It's also not ideal for seasoned Salesforce consultants who've been in the trenches for years and have battle scars to prove it (though you might enjoy a chuckle or two at familiar scenarios).

Lastly, if you're allergic to stick figure illustrations or have an aversion to occasional dad jokes, you might want to proceed with caution.

This book is meant to inform and entertain, and I make no apologies for injecting a little humour into the sometimes dry world of CRM implementation!

---

[2] For the purposes of this book, implementation partner, CRM partner, Salesforce partner and vendor are interchangeable.
[3] At age 4!

How is this book arranged?

I've structured this book to follow the natural flow of a new Salesforce implementation project.

The book begins with the basics - recognising the need for change and building a business case. Then we dive into the nitty-gritty of discovery and planning, before moving on to the actual implementation.

Finally, we cover the critical post-go-live phase and strategies for continuous improvement.

Each chapter begins with a snippet from DataNova's journey, bringing the concepts to life through relatable scenarios.

Then the chapter postscript breaks down the key learnings and best practices.

And because I can never resist sharing a good (or bad) war story, you'll find plenty of real-world anecdotes sprinkled throughout.

How did this book come about?

This book is the result of countless late nights, numerous cups of coffee, and perhaps a few too many "aha!" moments scribbled into my Google Keep app.

After years of seeing clients struggle with the same challenges project after project, I realised there was a gap in the resources available to them.

Sure, there are plenty of technical manuals out there, but what about a guide that speaks to the human side of CRM implementation? One that acknowledges the frustrations, celebrates the victories, and provides practical, actionable advice along the way?

That's what I set out to create. This book is my way of passing on the lessons I've learned - sometimes the hard way - to help you navigate your Salesforce implementation with confidence, clarity, and maybe even a bit of fun along the way.

If you're a consultant, you might want to get a copy (or 10!) of this book for your client to help set them up for success on their Salesforce journey!

I had a lot of great feedback on my previous book: Salesforce Discovery 101, especially the fact that it was an enjoyable and easy read. Following on from the same style and format, I hope that this book will also hit the mark.

So, grab a cup of your favourite beverage, get comfortable, and let's dive in. I am so glad you're here!

Customer Relationship Management systems such as Salesforce help organisations make better decision by centralising customer data and other information. Needless to say, this change isn't always welcome.
Which is why it is important to pay attention to the change management component of project delivery.

The Business Case

1
Recognising the Need for Change

Successful transformation begins with a candid assessment of where we are and why things aren't working so well anymore. Preferably before an accident happens and you end up with broken plates and broken bones everywhere. Metaphorically of course.

"I understand. I'm really sorry this happened. I'll be speaking to my team and we'll make sure that this doesn't happen again."

Azul's eyebrows were furrowed as she hung up the phone. She paused for a moment, tapping her finger idly on the table, deep in thought.

"Uungu, I think we need to do something about this. This is the third time in the last few weeks that different account execs have made sales outreach to the same people. Not good."

"Not good at all," she repeated, shaking her head in frustration.

The project manager had heard the tail end of her phone call and had paused the email he was crafting so he could focus on what she was saying.

Uungu nodded, stroking his purple goatee.

"I've noticed it too. It makes us look disorganised and unprofessional. We need a proper system to track our sales outreach efforts," he mused.

Azul leaned back on her chair and sighed.

"And when Hijau had that accident and was in the hospital for weeks, we just didn't know what was going on with his accounts."

She got up and paced the small conference room. "Uung, remember when we started DataNova and it was just the five of us? We'd just shout across the room if we had questions or needed to coordinate anything."

They looked at each other and cracked a smile, recalling some of the things they got up to when DataNova was in its foundling stage – such as the coffee dunking pizza incident.

"Right," Uungu shook his head, snapping himself out of the reverie. "We can't go back. It was ok to be scrappy in the beginning, but now that we've grown so much – our systems need to be able to scale as well."

"Let me dig into this situation a bit more and get back to you on what we should do next."

Azul nodded, grateful for Uungu's initiative. As Sales Director, she was constantly juggling multiple priorities, so it was crucial to have a team that she could depend on when she needed to delegate tasks.

* * *

DataNova was a well-regarded market intelligence company that delivered market research reports and customised intelligence solutions.

With his marketing background, Uungu initially joined DataNova to help with client outreach and brand management, but as the company grew – he found himself taking on more of a project management role, overseeing the delivery of complex research projects.

After his conversation with Azul, Uungu organised focus groups with sales reps, analysts and account managers to get an understanding of the situation.

He reviewed the current sales process with key stakeholders and found out that valuable client information is often lost or siloed within individual email accounts and random Google sheets.

"Pulling together a sales report for Azul every week is such a pain. I have to get everyone to update their stuff on their Google sheets, and then I have to collate the info and it just takes aaaages," Kijani the sales admin grumbled.

The team have been relying on a combination of Google sheets for tracking client interactions, shared Google drive folders for storing reports and client information and email for most of their communication.

While this approach worked in their early years, it was clear that this system has not scaled well.

Something had to change, and Uungu felt ready to help DataNova take the next step.

Organisational self-awareness

In my experience with CRM implementations, I've learned that successful transformation projects begin with an organisation's ability to recognise the need for a CRM system.

This recognition usually comes from being self-aware and identifying key pain points within their operations.

The following are three key practices that contribute to organisational self-awareness.

Conduct thorough internal assessments

Regular internal evaluations are essential for identifying areas that need improvement. It's a bit like getting regular physical health checks so that you know how to manage your lifestyle too.

To conduct effective internal assessments:

- Perform regular reviews of key performance indicators (KPIs) across departments
- Benchmark your organisation's performance against industry standards and competitors
- Analyse trends in customer complaints and feedback
- Review and map out current processes to identify inefficiencies
- Conduct regular technology audits to assess the effectiveness of current tools

Gather Comprehensive Feedback

Collecting input from various stakeholders provides invaluable insights into organisational needs. This cannot be a passive thing - a 'feedback box' will not do in this instance – it is the easy option, but will not get you the feedback and the valuable insight you are looking for.

To gather effective feedback:

- Implement systematic client feedback collection and analysis
- Create employee feedback loops through surveys and regular check-ins
- Conduct process audits to understand the customer journey - especially their emotional states as they go through the business process
- Run workshops or 'ride-along'/shadow sessions to understand internal processes and workflows[4]
- Perform post-project reviews to capture lessons learned
- Consider bringing in external consultants for an unbiased perspective

I've been involved in many projects where the leadership team assumed they knew what their team needed, providing requirements without validating with the actual users.

Systems like these often missed the mark in meeting users' real needs, leading to low adoption rates.

To avoid this, I emphasise the value of gathering comprehensive, bottom-up feedback as a critical part of understanding an organization's actual needs.

Listening closely to people on the front lines — those who face clients, constituents, patients, and customers daily — offers invaluable insights. Their firsthand experiences reveal the root of operational challenges and can be instrumental in designing effective solutions.

---

[4] This is sometimes known as DILO observations: a way of understanding someone's day-to-day functions by shadowing them and observing a "Day In the Life Of" a sales rep, a contact centre operative etc.

Foster a Culture of Open Communication

A culture that supports honest dialogue is crucial for identifying and addressing organisational challenges.

Here are some ways to promote open communication:

- Cultivate psychological safety, where employees can genuinely feel secure expressing concerns without fear of reprisal
- Encourage a growth mindset that views challenges as opportunities for improvement
- Prioritise transparency and integrity as core organisational values
- Implement regular town halls or open forums for discussion of organisational issues
- Recognise and reward employees who contribute to process improvements

Recognising the need for a CRM system is often the result of an organisation's willingness to ask difficult questions and face honest, candid answers, even if they might be unpalatable to hear.

This self-awareness not only helps in identifying the need for a CRM but also lays the groundwork for a successful implementation by ensuring that the chosen solution truly addresses the organisation's specific challenges and goals. Indeed, this will help any project where an element of change management is needed.

The Business Case

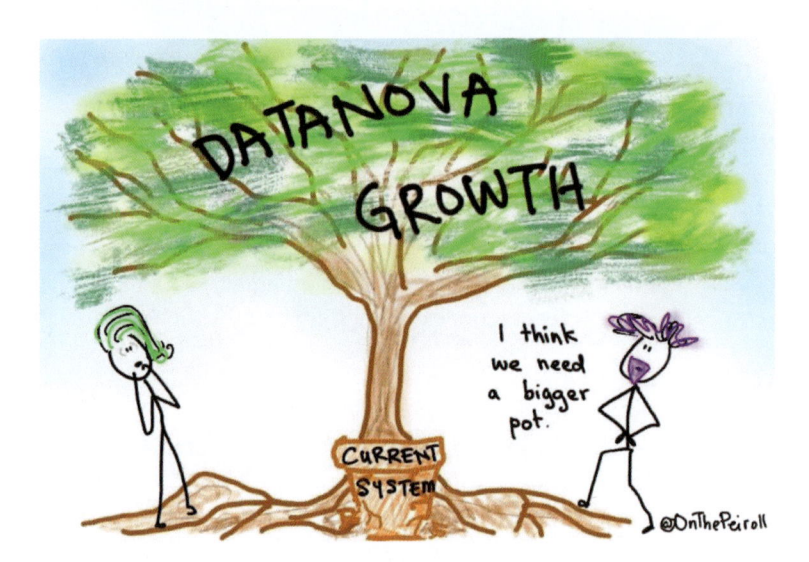

2
Crafting a Compelling Business Case

*When utilising design thinking in building business cases, it is pertinent to ask whether it is desirable, viable or feasible. Obviously in the case of DataNova, the answer is "Yes" to all three questions.
However, they are going to need some help to get there.*

The Business Case

Uungu leaned back on his chair, twirling his purple goatee absent-mindedly. The draft business plan was forming in his mind – a jumble of facts, figures and gut feelings.

He knew he had to provide a more compelling argument for implementing a new CRM system when presenting to the senior leadership team.

And so he spent the following morning huddling with Kijani, poring over reports and feedback from the internal assessments.

"Kijani, if you had a magic wand, what would you change about how we currently do things?" He chewed the back end of his pen.

She didn't hesitate for one moment. "Make reporting less of a nightmare. And stop us from tripping over each other with client outreach."

Uungu nodded, tapping away at his keyboard. In a few hours, they had a list of concrete objectives:

1. *Increase sales team productivity by 20% within six months[5]*
2. *Achieve 98% data accuracy in client records within three months*
3. *Reduce duplicate outreach incidents to zero within the first month*
4. *Decrease time spent on weekly sales reporting by 80%*
5. *Improve lead conversion rate by 15% within the first year*
6. *Achieve 90% user adoption rate within three months of go-live*

"Now that's something I can sell," Uungu smiled, looking at their list with satisfaction. "But how do we get there? Build it ourselves or bring in the experts?"

With objectives in hand, Uungu knew his next challenge was to put actual numbers to the benefits. He needed to speak the language of Return On Investment (ROI) to win over DataNova's Chief Financial Officer.

---

[5] To measure effectiveness of the new system, metrics and Key Performance Indicators (KPIs) would require these objectives to be defined. For example – what does productivity mean for the DataNova Sales team

He camped out in the finance department for two days, much to the amusement of the accountants. "Purple beard alert!" they'd call out whenever he appeared, asking for yet another report or clarification.

But it paid off. Armed with financial data and a newfound appreciation for spreadsheets, Uungu crunched the numbers:

- *Time savings: 5,200 hours per year across the sales team*
- *Productivity gains: $260,000 annually* [6]
- *Increased sales from improved conversion: $750,000 in additional revenue*

'Wow, this isn't half bad," Uungu said, eyebrows raised.

But then came the tricky part: comparing the costs and benefits of building in-house versus hiring an external partner.

He did some preliminary investigations and spoke to a few Salesforce partners for a high-level estimate based on DataNova's outline requirements[7]*.*

In-house option (where he would have to train or hire experienced people):

- *Total first-year cost: $300,000*
- *Timeline: 10 months*
- *First-year ROI: 93%*

External partner option:

- *Total first-year cost: $300,000 (including $40,000 for the discovery from two partners)*
- *Timeline: 5 months*
- *First-year ROI: 93%*

---

[6] A sample Business Case for DataNova can be found in the Appendix, where you'll get an idea of how these numbers might be calculated.

[7] These high-level estimates provided during pre-sales discussions should be taken conservatively, as additional details uncovered during deeper discussions during discoveries will be able to provide a more firm and clearer idea of requirements and costings.

Uungu scratched his head. "Same costs, same ROI... but we get there twice as fast with a partner. Interesting."[8]

It was essential for Uungu to choose the right partner, which was why he was proposing that two Salesforce partners conduct their own discovery workshops.

This approach would allow each partner to present more comprehensive proposals, enabling DataNova to compare both the technical implementation details and the commercial strategies.

Additionally, the discovery phase would provide insights into the human aspects of the relationship, such as working styles, which would allow DataNova to make a more informed decision when selecting a long-term partner.

This meant an additional $20,000 per partner would need to be added to the External Partner option in the business case but Uungu felt that this was an investment that would be worthwhile[9].

* * *

Uungu knew that no proposal was complete without addressing the risks and could already hear Azul's voice in his head: "But what if it all goes wrong?"

To tackle this, Uungu decided to host a "Worst-Case Scenario" lunch. He invited team leads from Sales, IT, and Customer Service, promising free pizza in exchange for their darkest CRM implementation fears.

The session was both productive and slightly terrifying.

Uungu's whiteboard soon filled with potential disasters for both the in-house and external partner options:

- "What if we can't hire the right Salesforce team?"

---

[8] In real life, such numbers are rarely this convenient and tidy, so please allow me some creative license to aid the storytelling process.

[9] I have seen this happen once in all my years of consulting. A previous client engaged two vendors to run discovery workshops and present a demo and proposal for the two competing CRM platforms: Salesforce and Microsoft Dynamics CRM. While Salesforce won on features – ultimately Microsoft's license deal for 3-years made a far more compelling business case for the client.

- *"What if the external partner doesn't understand our unique needs?"*
- *"What if the sales team hates it and refuses to use it?"*

As the pizza disappeared, so did the panic. For each risk, the team brainstormed mitigation strategies.

Uungu left with a comprehensive risk assessment and mitigation plan, as well as a slight case of pepperonitis, or too-many-pepperoni-slices.

He carefully crafted a risk matrix, comparing the in-house and external partner options.

Risk	In-House	External Partner	Mitigation Strategy
Implementation Failure	High	Low	Have two partners run discovery in parallel so that we have two proposals to choose and compare
Timeline Overrun	High	Medium	Develop detailed project plan with buffers; monitor progress closely
Budget Overrun	Medium	Medium	Maintain detailed budget tracking; include contingency fund
Poor User Adoption	Medium	Low	Comprehensive change management and training plan
Data Migration Issues	High	Medium	Thorough data cleansing and validation process

Uungu sat back, looking at his completed analysis.

The evidence was clear: while both options had merit, the external partner approach offered faster implementation, lower risk, and access to specialised expertise.

The Analysis

In case I was a little too subtle, this part of the story has been simplified to illustrate the basic foundation of creating a business case.

This process could have been a two-stepped approach; first to determine if CRM is the solution to the problem they are experiencing, and second to evaluate options for how to implement the solution[10].

As you can see from the narrative above, crafting a successful business case is both an art and a science.

A well-structured business case is crucial for gaining approval and support for significant initiatives within an organisation.

I can't tell you how often I've been involved in project implementations that do not have a solid business case.

Also, please bear in mind that business cases are rarely as tidy and neat as that in the DataNova story.

Sometimes the cost for engaging an external partner might be a more expensive option, but might still be a preferable option based on other factors – such as how quickly you might need the system or your ability to find and retain the right talent.

The right option will depend on many factors, but the thoughtful process of writing up a robust business case will allow you to evaluate the options carefully in order to arrive at the right decision for your situation.

So, how do we make sure that we are able to create a persuasive argument for the proposed project or change?

---

[10] Actually, you could argue that there should really be an additional step to decide which CRM system would be the most suitable platform. For the purposes of this book, I am taking the creative license to shortcut this process and have them select Salesforce as the platform of choice.

The Power of Clear Objectives

The foundation of any strong business case is a clear set of objectives and expected outcomes. This provides a roadmap for the entire project and ensures all stakeholders are aligned.

To effectively define objectives and outcomes:

- Use SMART criteria (Specific, Measurable, Achievable, Relevant, Time-bound) when setting goals
- Align objectives with broader organisational strategies and goals. For example, a company having a premium, niche and bespoke offering would have a different strategy than if they focused on volume and commodity
- Involve key stakeholders in the objective-setting process to ensure buy-in
- Clearly articulate how success will be measured

Without clear objectives, projects can lack direction, leading to scope creep[11], wasted resources, and difficulty in evaluating success.

Pro-tip: Implementing Salesforce because the only reason for it is that the new Sales Director has used it in their previous company does not make a good business case![12]

Quantify Potential Benefits (ROI and Efficiency Gains)

Numbers speak louder than words when it comes to convincing decision-makers. Quantifying the potential benefits of your proposal is crucial for building a compelling case.

To effectively quantify benefits:

- Conduct a thorough cost-benefit analysis

---

[11] Scope creep is the uncontrolled expansion of project scope beyond original parameters. See Appendix for Glossary.
[12] Unfortunately, newcomers to leadership team within an organisation will usually want to make their mark by initiating new projects without building a strong business case to back it up. That usually leads to a sub-par implementation that makes for good anecdotes!

- Calculate expected Return on Investment (ROI)
- Estimate efficiency gains in terms of time or resources saved
- Project potential revenue increases or cost savings
- Use historical data and industry benchmarks to support your calculations

Failing to quantify benefits can make it difficult to justify the investment and may lead to your proposal being seen as a "nice to have" rather than a critical initiative.

What's really important is to articulate all the assumptions made when quantifying the benefits as well as the costs.

For example – efficiency gains may depend on 100% user adoption rate, but is that realistic?

Address risks and mitigation strategies

Every project comes with risks. Acknowledging these upfront and proposing mitigation strategies demonstrates foresight and preparedness.

To effectively address risks:

- Conduct a comprehensive risk assessment
- Categorise risks (e.g., financial, operational, technical)
- Estimate the likelihood and potential impact of each risk
- Develop specific mitigation strategies for high-priority risks
- Create contingency plans for potential issues

Neglecting to address risks can lead to unexpected challenges derailing the project and may cause stakeholders to lose confidence in the initiative.

You should create a Risk Register or a RAIDD[13] log right at the beginning of the business case inception and review it with key project team members regularly throughout the life of the project.

---

[13] RAIDD log: A document that lists down the Risks, Assumptions, Issues, Dependencies and Decisions that impact the project. See Appendix for Glossary.

The Business Case

One final note about the business case – it's not a one and done activity. The project team should revisit the business case at key points in the project to ask if it is still valid.

An example of when a business case for a Salesforce implementation may no longer be valid – could be when companies go through mergers or acquisitions, or when regulatory or compliance change happens (such as Brexit, which was a traumatic event for us in the UK!)

It pays to pay attention to having a strong "WHY", i.e. business for the project to set it up for success.

The exercise of calculating the ROI (Return On Investment) should be done with honesty and integrity. I've seen a biased business case where costs where ignored, leading to an implementation that did not bring the promised ROI.

3
Securing Executive Buy-In

Securing executive buy-in begins with empathy, delivering a strong and compelling argument with persuasive skills.

Uungu stood outside the boardroom, taking a moment to collect his thoughts. He smoothed his shirt, more out of habit than necessity, and took a deep breath to centre himself.

In his hands, he held a sleek folder containing his meticulously prepared presentation. Today was the day he would present his CRM implementation plan to DataNova's executive team.

As he entered the room, Uungu took in the faces around the table.

There was Azul, the Sales Director, who had first highlighted their systemic issues.

Next to her sat Amarillo, or Amar as he preferred to be called, the CTO whose responsibilities included all things IT at DataNova.

Hoong, the CFO was also there. He was known for his keen financial acumen and ability to dissect projections with surgical precision.

And finally, there was Zambarau, or Zamba, the CEO, her presence commanding attention even in silence, her calm gaze fixed on Uungu.

Uungu began, his voice steady. "Thank you all for your time. Today, I'm going to demonstrate how a new CRM system can transform our client relationships and significantly impact our bottom line."

He had crafted his presentation to address each executive's specific concerns, shifting his focus seamlessly as he progressed through his slides.

Turning to Hoong, Uungu delved into the financials. "By implementing this CRM system with an external partner, we're projecting a first-year ROI of 93%. That translates to over half a million dollars in net benefit within the first twelve months."

Hoong nodded, his interest piqued.

Uungu then addressed Amar, highlighting the technical advantages.

"Amar, I know integration and scalability are top priorities for you. This system will be able to integrate with the report and document generation systems we are looking to implement in the near future. It's built on a flexible platform that can grow with us, and it offers robust security features to safeguard our sensitive client data."

Amar nodded, his earlier restlessness replaced by keen interest.

Finally, Uungu addressed the CEO directly.

"Zamba, this isn't just about streamlining our internal processes. This CRM implementation will position us as an industry leader. We'll be able to offer a level of personalised service that our competitors can't match, aligning perfectly with your vision for DataNova's future."

Zamba leaned forward, her expression thoughtful and intrigued.

Throughout his presentation, Uungu bolstered his arguments with data and industry benchmarks. He knew these executives needed hard facts, not vague promises.

"Recent industry reports show that companies in our sector implementing similar CRM systems have seen an average 25% increase in customer retention rates," Uungu said, moving to a new slide.

"For us, that could mean an additional $1.2 million in recurring revenue annually."

He continued, "Moreover, a case study of a comparable company showed that post-CRM implementation, they reduced their sales cycle by 15%, leading to faster closures and increased revenue."

The executives exchanged impressed glances.

Hoong was taking copious notes, while Amar had set aside his tablet, giving Uungu his undivided attention. Zamba's expression remained neutral, but her eyes sparkled with interest.

As he neared his conclusion, Uungu knew it was time to address potential objections head-on. He had anticipated every possible counterargument and prepared thoughtful responses.

"I understand you might have some concerns," Uungu said.

"So let's address them directly."

Hoong voiced the question Uungu had anticipated. "This sounds promising, Uungu, and I like your discussion comparing the in-house and external partner approach. You're recommending that we engage the external partner but you propose running two discoveries so that we can compare their proposals. Isn't this a costly move?"

Uungu was prepared. "I appreciate that concern, Hoong. I strongly believe in finding the right partner that we can trust in the long term, and I feel that this investment will pay for itself over time."

He displayed a slide showing a detailed breakdown of the roadmap and potential cost savings.

Hoong leaned in, scrutinising the numbers.

Uungu continued, addressing another likely objection. "Amar, you might be concerned about potential disruption to our current operations during implementation. I've drafted a comprehensive change management strategy to ensure a smooth transition, including thorough training and support for our team."

Amar nodded appreciatively. "You've clearly given this a lot of thought, Uungu. I'm impressed."

As Uungu concluded his presentation, he could sense a shift in the room's energy. The leadership team was genuinely excited!

Zamba spoke, her voice carrying authority. "This is impressive work, Uungu. You've clearly done your due diligence and addressed our key concerns. I think we all agree this merits serious consideration."

She looked around the table, receiving nods of agreement from the other executives. "Let's reconvene next week to discuss next steps. Excellent job, Uungu."

Uungu allowed himself a little smile of relief. He had cleared the first major hurdle – securing that crucial executive buy-in.

The journey was far from over, but he had overcome a significant obstacle. DataNova was one step closer to transforming its client relationships and solidifying its position in the competitive market intelligence industry.

Delivering a Compelling Presentation

Gaining executive approval is crucial for implementing significant initiatives within an organisation.

Without strong buy-in from leadership, even the most promising projects can languish, failing to deliver their intended benefits. And let's be honest – that's a waste of time, money, and potential that no organisation can afford.

In my years as a consultant and project manager, I've seen countless great ideas fall by the wayside due to a lack of executive support[14].

On the flip side, I've also seen how a well-crafted, persuasive presentation can turn sceptical executives into passionate advocates.

Here are some strategies I've found effective in creating presentations that resonate with decision-makers and secure their support.

Tailor your presentation to your audience

Understanding and addressing the specific interests and priorities of each executive is fundamental to a successful pitch. It's not just about presenting information – it's about making that information relevant and compelling to each individual in the room.

To effectively tailor your presentation:

- Research each executive's background, responsibilities, and key concerns
- Adjust the level of detail and technical jargon based on each executive's expertise
- Find out what style works better for each executive, e.g. storytelling vs graphs
- Highlight aspects of your proposal that align with each executive's goals and priorities

---

[14] Here's an interesting article on why CRM projects fail:
https://www.salesforce.com/ap/hub/crm/why-do-crm-projects-fail/

- Prepare specific talking points that address potential questions or concerns from each executive
- Use language and metaphors that resonate with each executive's communication style

Empathy is key here. If you can't see things from your audience's perspective, you're unlikely to understand why they might not immediately grasp or agree with your point of view. Put yourself in their shoes – what would you need to hear to be convinced?

It's also important to get the right balance, because when you try to please everyone, you please no one.

It's worth noting that sometimes dominant voices in the room might drown out women and people from under-represented backgrounds who may not get an opportunity to be heard.

Make sure you create a space for them to share their voice as well.

Use data to support your arguments

While successful influence often hinges on emotions, having solid data to back up your proposal lends credibility to your arguments and helps quantify the potential benefits of your initiative.

In my experience, a well-placed statistic or case study (or a well-placed tray of donuts!) can often be the tipping point in winning over a sceptical executive. I have been known to use bribery when it suited me!

If bribery is not to your taste, here are some other ways you might approach this:

- Do your research to find relevant industry reports and statistics
- Prepare case studies of similar implementations in your industry or comparable organisations
- Use visual aids such as charts and graphs to make data more digestible
- Provide specific, quantifiable projections for key metrics relevant to your organisation
- Be prepared to explain the sources and methodology behind your data

It's crucial to be able to justify your recommendations, which is why it pays to go the extra mile in acquiring solid data to support your proposal.

For example: "According to a 2022 IDC study commissioned by Salesforce, organisations using Salesforce Customer 360 saw an average five-year ROI of 271%. The study was based on interviews with 13 organisations using Salesforce Customer 360 applications."

Remember, executives are often bombarded with ideas and proposals – your data needs to be compelling enough to cut through the noise.

Anticipate and address potential objections

Proactively identifying and preparing responses to likely concerns or counterarguments demonstrates thoroughness and builds confidence in your proposal.

Have a pow-wow, or a worst-case scenario pizza luncheon – whatever works, to get the team to share their nightmares and fears. Then brainstorm ways to address and mitigate them.

This shows that you're not just an ideas person, but someone who has thought through the practicalities of implementation.

To effectively address potential objections before your meeting:

- Brainstorm possible concerns from each executive's perspective
- Conduct a thorough risk assessment of your proposal
- Develop mitigation strategies for identified risks
- Prepare concise, fact-based responses to potential objections
- Consider alternative solutions or compromises for major concerns
- Practice addressing objections in a non-defensive, collaborative manner

The last point is particularly important. For some people, hearing objections to their idea may trigger a defensive response, which can derail the discussion. I'll admit, it's something I've struggled with myself at times.

What I've learned to do is to mentally separate myself from my proposal. I remind myself that objections and criticisms aren't a judgment on me as a person, but an opportunity to refine and improve the idea.

This mindset shift allows me to engage in a more productive manner, turning potential conflicts into collaborative problem-solving sessions. It helps me to shift focus back to the business and not my personal feelings or doubts.

A respected peer has some words of wisdom on this topic: "One thing I like to remind myself is that you need to aggressively seek out and uncover these objections. An unspoken and unaddressed objection from an exec can easily ruin your efforts. It's uncomfortable, but getting these out and addressed will help you in the long run."

Taking the time to thoroughly prepare in these areas can make the difference between a transformative success and a missed opportunity.

I've seen it happen time and time again – the projects that succeed are often not just the ones with the best ideas, but the ones that were presented in a way that truly resonated with the decision-makers.

At the end of the day, executives are people too. They have their own goals, pressures, and concerns. Your job is to show them how your proposal aligns with their objectives and addresses their worries.

Do that effectively, and you'll be well on your way to turning your vision into reality.

4
Preparing the Request for Proposal (RFP)

Fuzzy wuzzy fluffy requirements in RFPs often invite trouble. Hire management consultants to help get clarity if necessary, or be ready for a bumpy project!

Uungu leaned back in his chair, allowing himself a moment of quiet satisfaction.

With executive buy-in secured, the next challenge was developing a Request for Proposal (RFP) that would attract the right Salesforce implementation partners to bid specifically for the discovery phase and, based on that, submit detailed proposals for the full implementation.

"Team," Uungu addressed the small group gathered in the conference room, "We've got the green light from Zamba and the executive team. Now we need to find the right partner to turn this CRM vision into reality."

Azul nodded, her sales director instincts evident. "Clarity is key here. We can't afford any misinterpretations."

"Agreed," Uungu said. He turned to the whiteboard and wrote "Scope and Requirements" in bold letters.

"First, we need to define what we want this CRM to accomplish for us. It is important that we are clear about what we want."

Over the next few days, Uungu orchestrated a series of meetings with various stakeholders.

He sat down with Azul, the Sales Director, to understand the sales team's specific needs.

"We need a system that can handle our complex sales cycles and provide real-time visibility into our pipeline," Azul emphasised.

Kijani, representing the account managers, added, "And we need robust account management features. Our client relationships are key to our success."

Uungu made sure to include Hoong, the CFO, in discussions about financial reporting requirements and ROI expectations.

By involving these stakeholders, Uungu ensured that the RFP would address the real needs of those who would be using the system daily.

The team outlined their requirements, covering everything from basic contact management to managing the sales process and advanced reporting needs. Uungu ensured each requirement was specific, measurable, and aligned with their overall objectives.

"Remember," Uungu reminded the team, "anything not stated in the RFP is potentially out of scope. We need to be thorough."

By day's end, they had compiled a comprehensive list of requirements, categorised into must-haves and nice-to-haves.

* * *

The next morning, Uungu reconvened the team. "Today, we'll define how we'll evaluate the proposals we receive."

Hoong, the CFO, had joined for this session. "We need to ensure we're making fair comparisons," he said. "Clear evaluation criteria will facilitate that."

Uungu nodded. "Agreed. Let's create a scoring system for different aspects of the proposals."

They spent the afternoon defining criteria and assigning weights to each. Technical capability, industry experience, project timeline, and cost were all factored in. They also included criteria for evaluating the quality of the discovery.

As the day wore on and the RFP document took shape, Hijau, one of Kijani's counterparts, brought up a crucial point. "We should have the legal team review this before we send it out. There might be some contractual or compliance issues we haven't considered."

Uungu slapped his forehead. "Of course! Great catch, Jau. I'll schedule a meeting with the legal team first thing tomorrow."

The next day, Uungu sat down with Indigo, DataNova's lead counsel. Indigo's sharp eyes scanned the document, occasionally pausing to make notes or ask questions.

"You've done a good job outlining the technical requirements," he said, "but we need to strengthen the confidentiality clauses and add a clause about intellectual property rights."

Uungu listened intently as Indigo explained the reasons behind some of his proposed amendments to the RFP and the legal terms and conditions.

He realised that without this review, they could have exposed DataNova to unnecessary risks or legal complications down the line.

After incorporating Indigo's suggestions and making a few final tweaks, the RFP was ready.

As the week concluded, Uungu reviewed the final draft of the RFP with satisfaction. It was comprehensive, clear, and designed to attract the right partners.

"Great job, team," he said. "This RFP is our blueprint for selecting the right Salesforce partner. It clearly defines our needs and the criteria we'll use to evaluate potential partners."

Azul smiled, "I'm looking forward to seeing the proposals we receive."

Uungu nodded in agreement. "Indeed. The real work is just beginning, but with this RFP, we're setting ourselves up for success."

As the team dispersed, Uungu took a final look at the document on his laptop. DataNova's journey to revolutionise its client relationships was well underway.

Crafting an Effective RFP

An RFP – or a Request for Proposal is a formal document issued by a company seeking bids from vendors or service providers for a specific project or solution. It outlines the project requirements, goals and evaluation criteria, allowing vendors to submit detailed proposals on how they would meet those needs.

The goal of an RFP is to compare offers and select the best fit.

As such, it is important that the RFP be well-structured to attract the right vendors and set the stage for a successful project.

Throughout my career, I've seen my fair share of poorly written RFPs, and it's not hard to see why some projects go off the rails before they even start.

Here are some key elements to focus on when crafting an RFP.

Engaging Key Stakeholders

Engaging key stakeholders in the RFP process ensures that the document accurately reflects the organisation's needs and sets the stage for high user adoption. To effectively identify and engage stakeholders:

- Conduct focused sessions with business leadership (such as sales/service/marketing directors) to understand strategic goals
- Gather input from sales representatives and account managers about their day-to-day needs
- Include finance team members to ensure alignment with reporting and ROI expectations
- Create a cross-functional team to review and approve the final RFP
- Use stakeholder input to prioritize requirements and set realistic project expectations

I've seen projects falter simply because a key stakeholder was overlooked, or their concerns weren't adequately addressed.

Failing to identify and engage key stakeholders can lead to resistance to change, misaligned expectations, and ultimately, project failure.

Include evaluation criteria in the RFP

Providing clear evaluation criteria in your RFP helps vendors understand your priorities and allows for more accurate comparison of proposals. Here's how to effectively include evaluation criteria:

- Define specific criteria for assessing technical capability, experience, cost, and other relevant factors
- Assign weights to different criteria based on their importance to your project
- Consider including a scoring rubric to make the evaluation process transparent
- Specify any minimum qualifications or "deal-breaker" criteria
- Include criteria for evaluating the quality of vendor presentations or discovery sessions, if applicable

Failing to include clear evaluation criteria can lead to difficulties in comparing proposals objectively, potential bias in the selection process, and the risk of choosing a vendor that isn't the best fit for your needs.

One more crucial point – be upfront about any aggressive timelines and their reasons. For example, if you need to decommission a legacy system due to licence expiry issues that could incur financial penalties, make that clear.

Get the legal team to review RFP

A legal review of your RFP is a critical step that's often overlooked or rushed. Having your legal team review the document can protect your organisation from potential risks and ensure compliance with relevant laws and regulations. Here's how to effectively incorporate legal review into your RFP process:

- Schedule the legal review early in the RFP development process

- Provide context to the legal team about the project's goals and any industry-specific considerations
- Ask the legal team to pay special attention to intellectual property rights, confidentiality clauses, and liability issues
- Incorporate legal feedback into the RFP and have the legal team review the final draft
- Allow sufficient time for the legal review to avoid rushing this crucial step

Skipping or rushing the legal review can lead to serious consequences.

Without proper legal review, you risk including terms that may not be enforceable, overlooking important protections for your organisation, or even inadvertently disclosing sensitive information.

In the worst-case scenario, you could end up in legal disputes with vendors or face compliance issues that could have been easily avoided.

Now, I understand why RFPs are important in evaluating vendors, but I'll be honest – I don't believe they're always the best way to do so.

I believe that it can be more useful to engage partners for small projects such as pilots and proof of concepts to evaluate ways of working and cultural fit. This allows a foundation of trust to be built so that a long-term partnership can be established.

However, I recognise that many organisations have policies that require RFPs to be used for vendor procurement. If that's the case, then it's crucial to make sure it's done right. Otherwise, it's a waste of money and time – for all parties involved.

Taking the time to craft a thoughtful, comprehensive RFP can make the difference between a challenging project with misaligned expectations and a smooth, successful implementation that meets your organisation's needs. It's not just about finding a vendor – it's about finding the right partner who can help bring your vision to life.

Remember, the RFP is often the first impression a potential partner gets of your organisation and project. Make it count. Be clear, be thorough, and be open to dialogue. Your future self (and your future implementation partner) will thank you for it.

Discovery & Planning

5
Preparing for Partner Engagement

Strong project governance is frequently overlooked because it 'slows down progress' but is key to ensuring projects don't go off the rails.

As Uungu entered Zamba's office for their weekly catch-up, he knew it was time to establish a formal governance structure for the project.

"Zamba," he began, "we need to set up a steering committee for the CRM project. I believe we need representation from Sales, IT, Finance, and Marketing at a minimum."

Zamba leaned back, considering. "Agreed. Who do you have in mind?"

Uungu laid out his proposal: Azul for Sales, Amar for IT, Hoong for Finance, and Jade for Marketing, with Zamba herself as the executive sponsor. "And once we complete the discovery phase and select our implementation partner, we'll need their representation on the committee as well," he added.

They discussed the committee's responsibilities: approving major decisions, resolving high-level issues, and ensuring the project remained aligned with DataNova's strategic goals.

"What about day-to-day decisions?" Zamba inquired.

Uungu was prepared. He proposed a tiered decision-making framework: the project team would handle routine decisions, he as the project manager would manage medium-impact choices, and only significant issues or changes would be escalated to the steering committee.

Zamba nodded her approval. "You've clearly thought this through. Set it up."

As Uungu left Zamba's office, he encountered Kijani in the hallway. The sales team lead looked concerned.

"Uungu, my team's getting anxious about this project. They're hearing rumours about massive changes coming."

Uungu realised it was time to accelerate his change management and communication plan.

He called an impromptu meeting with Azul and Jade.

"We need a comprehensive change management and communication plan," Uungu began.

Azul raised her right eyebrow. "What do you have in mind?"

"First, regular updates to all staff," Uungu said. "We'll use email, the intranet, and monthly calls."

Jade nodded. "We could also create a project intranet site for FAQs and updates."

"Great idea," Uungu agreed. "And let's identify 'CRM Champions' in each department as liaison points."

"What about training?" Azul asked.

"We'll start with a skills assessment," Uungu replied. "Then we'll develop a phased training plan aligned with the implementation timeline."

"We should also create 'day in the life' scenarios," Jade suggested. "Help staff envision how Salesforce will improve their work."

"Perfect," Uungu said. "And let's set up a recognition program for early adopters and power users."

Uungu worked into the evening on the change management programme, driven by determination and perhaps a bit too much coffee.

Tomorrow he would turn his attention to preparing the internal team for partner collaboration. He knew that working effectively with an external partner would be crucial for the project's success.

* * *

The next morning, Uungu gathered his core team in the conference room. As they settled in, he could sense a mix of excitement and apprehension in the air.

"Team," Uungu began, his voice carrying a note of enthusiasm, "we're about to embark on a journey with our CRM implementation partner. But before we do, we need to make sure we're ready to collaborate effectively."

Azul leaned forward, her brow furrowed. "What exactly does that mean, Uungu? We've worked with consultants before."

Uungu nodded, acknowledging her point. "True, but this is different. We're not just bringing in short-term help. We're entering into a partnership that will shape the future of our sales operations."

He turned to the whiteboard and started sketching out a diagram. "Imagine our team and the partner's team as two gears. For the project to run smoothly, these gears need to mesh perfectly."

Kijani chimed in, "And if they don't?"

"Friction, delays, misunderstandings," Uungu replied. "We've all seen projects go sideways because of poor collaboration."

He outlined his plan for a series of internal calls to prepare the team. As he described each element, he could see the team becoming more engaged.

What followed was a lively back-and-forth, with the rest of the team chiming in with suggestions. By the end of the exercise, everyone was feeling positive and energised.

As the meeting wound down, Jade spoke up. "You know, I was sceptical about needing 'preparation' to work with a partner. But now I see how crucial this is."

Uungu nodded, pleased. "Exactly. By investing this time now, we're setting ourselves up for a much smoother collaboration."

As the team filed out, chatting excitedly about the upcoming workshops, Uungu felt a sense of accomplishment. They were not just preparing for a CRM implementation; they were preparing to be true partners in the process.

He turned back to his notes, already planning the next steps.

The plan for tomorrow was to meet the Cloudacious team to kick off the discovery phase. Thanks to their preparation, DataNova was ready for this crucial next step in their CRM journey.

Setting Up Partner Engagement for Success

Establishing a Governance Framework

What do you do when things go wrong? How do you anticipate issues and navigate around them before you crash into the metaphorical iceberg?

That's why it's crucial to have a clear governance structure and decision-making framework that provides clarity on roles, responsibilities, and processes for making project-related decisions.

Clear governance frameworks set up project implementation for success – whether you are executing the project with your own team or engaging external partners to help you do it.

To establish an effective governance and decision-making framework:

- Form a steering committee with representatives from key departments and the consulting partner
- Define the steering committee's responsibilities, meeting frequency, and decision-making authority
- Create a tiered decision-making process for different levels of project decisions
- Establish clear escalation paths for issue resolution
- Document and communicate the governance structure to all project stakeholders

Having a strong executive sponsor to push the project forward and find a way to navigate obstacles is critical to its success.

Lack of a clear decision-making framework within projects often leads to unnecessary delays as simple issues can bounce between departments with no clear resolution path.

Without a well-defined governance structure, projects can suffer from delayed decisions, unclear accountability, and misaligned priorities.

Planning for Change Management and Communication

Change management and communication are often underestimated but are critical for user adoption and overall project success.

A comprehensive plan helps manage expectations, address concerns, and build enthusiasm for the new system.

To develop an effective change management and communication plan:

- Create a detailed communication strategy with regular updates through various channels
- Identify "change champions" within each department to advocate for the project
- Conduct a skills assessment to identify training needs across the organisation
- Develop a phased training plan aligned with the implementation timeline
- Create "day in the life" scenarios to help staff envision how the new system will improve their work
- Establish a feedback mechanism to address concerns and gather suggestions throughout the project
- Consider how a stakeholder analysis might influence the different levels and types of communication used

I've seen projects with brilliant technical implementations fail spectacularly due to poor change management.

The leadership and project team are usually so caught up with the exciting features and capabilities of the new system that they forget about the people who would actually be using it – the users.

Change management is often an afterthought, and haphazard training alongside poorly coordinated communication is rarely enough to engage the users into adopting the system in a wholehearted way.

Preparing the Internal Team for Partner Collaboration

Effective collaboration with the implementation partner is crucial for project success. This is a step that is often overlooked, to the detriment of the project.

To prepare your internal team for partner collaboration:

- Conduct sessions on best practices for vendor management and collaboration
- Establish clear roles and responsibilities for internal team members during the partner engagement
- Set up processes for knowledge sharing and documentation
- Create guidelines for effective communication with the partner team
- Provide training on any collaboration tools that will be used during the project

By focusing on these key elements - governance, change management and preparation - organisations can create a solid foundation for their IT implementation projects.

This approach not only increases the likelihood of project success, but also sets the stage for a productive partnership with external consultants.

These activities are ongoing processes that continue throughout the project lifecycle. Regularly revisiting and refining your approach in these areas can help navigate challenges, maintain momentum, and ultimately deliver a successful implementation that meets organisational needs and gains widespread adoption.

In my years of experience, I've found that the projects that succeed are often not just the ones with the best technical solutions, but those that effectively manage the human element.

Technology might be at the core of what we're implementing, but at the end of the day, it's people who will be using it. Keeping that perspective front and centre can make all the difference in your project's success.

Discovery & Planning

*A high trust relationship with business partners will withstand some of the tough project challenges that can present themselves.
It pays to take the time to nurture and cultivate this relationship.*

Discovery & Planning

6
Analysis and Requirements Gathering

Fred's Law of Scope Creep says:
"Scope expands to consume any and all donuts of requirements that is offered to it." (A play on Parkinson's Law of Data: "Data expands to fill the storage available.")

Discovery & Planning

Uungu surveyed the conference room quietly, stroking his purple goatee between finger and thumb, with a look of concentration furrowed across his brows.

The Cloudacious team was there - Clem, the Business Analyst; Coco, the Solution Architect; and Vi, the Project Manager. They occupied one side of the table and across from them sat key DataNova stakeholders: Azul from Sales, Jade from Marketing, and Amar from IT.

They'd just returned from a small break after the discovery project kick-off, where introductions were made and expectations set, including roles and responsibilities.

Clem began facilitating a workshop on DataNova's current sales process, asking probing questions and sketching a process flow on the whiteboard.

As Azul outlined the sales workflow, Uungu noticed Kijani, the sales team lead, shifting uncomfortably.

"Kijani," Uungu prompted gently, "you seem to have something to add."

Kijani hesitated before speaking. "Well, that's the official process, but in practice, we often use workarounds because the current system is so cumbersome."

This sparked a lively discussion, with team members from various departments highlighting inefficiencies and pain points.

As they wrapped up the current state mapping for this process, Coco took the floor to demonstrate some of Salesforce's capabilities that could address these issues.

Uungu observed his colleagues' growing excitement, particularly Jade from Marketing, who was enthused about integrated campaign management possibilities.

"Let's pause for a moment," Uungu interjected, noting the building enthusiasm. "Coco, can you clarify what's standard functionality versus what might require more complex customisation?"

As Coco explained, Uungu jotted down notes, already beginning to mentally categorise these potential requirements. He knew that

Discovery & Planning

prioritisation would be an ongoing process throughout the discovery phase.

"Great insights, everyone," Uungu said as they wrapped up for the day. "Remember, we're still in the early stages of discovery. We'll be continually refining our understanding of what's needed and what's possible as we progress."

* * *

The next day, as they delved into another process, Uungu reminded the team, "As we uncover more about our needs and Salesforce's capabilities, let's keep thinking about priorities. Not everything can be a 'must-have' for the initial phase."

Throughout the week, Uungu regularly conferred with Vi to review the emerging requirements against the original RFP.

"We're uncovering a lot during these workshops," Uungu noted. "Some of these potential requirements weren't in the initial RFP. We need to keep prioritising as we go."

They began to loosely categorise requirements using the MoSCoW[15] method, knowing that these categories might shift as they learned more.

As the discovery workshops continued, Uungu consistently balanced ambition with practicality, always keeping an eye on the evolving list of potential requirements and their relative importance.

"This is an ongoing process," he reminded everyone. "We'll keep refining our priorities as we learn more about our needs and the system's capabilities. By the end of discovery, we'll have a clear, prioritised list of requirements to guide our implementation."

* * *

In parallel to the discovery workshops Cloudacious was running, Uungu turned his focus on the crucial issue of data preparation. He knew this workstream needed to start as soon as possible to ensure

---

[15] MoSCoW is a method for prioritising requirements and is an acronym that stands for "Must have", "Should have", "Could have", and "Won't have (right now)".

clean, deduplicated data would be ready for migration when the implementation phase began.

He arranged a meeting with Amar and Kijani. "We need to discuss our data situation and start planning our cleansing strategy," Uungu said, his tone serious.

Amar sighed. "I was anticipating this. Our data is... in a less-than-ideal state."

Kijani nodded in agreement. "We've got contact information spread across multiple Google Sheets and mailboxes, and our opportunity data is all over the place."

They spent the following week assessing DataNova's current data landscape, identifying sources scattered across numerous spreadsheets, and legacy systems.

Meanwhile, Coco from Cloudacious was running data mapping workshops to design the target data model for Salesforce. Uungu made sure to attend these sessions, knowing the insights gained would be crucial for the data cleansing effort.

After one such workshop, Uungu huddled with his team. "Based on what we've learned about the Salesforce data model, we need to start consolidating our contact and opportunity data into standardised formats. This will make the eventual migration much smoother."

Uungu assembled a dedicated team for the data cleansing initiative, facing some initial resistance from colleagues who viewed it as menial work.

"This data is the foundation of our operations," Uungu explained. "Clean data means better insights, improved customer satisfaction, and ultimately, greater success for all of us. And remember, we need to have this done before the actual implementation begins, so we're on a tight timeline."

Uungu established a systematic approach:

- *Consolidate all sales contact lists into a single master spreadsheet*
- *Standardise company names and contact information fields*
- *Identify and merge duplicate contacts*

Discovery & Planning

- Compile all opportunity information into a standardised format
- Clean and validate product and pricing data

Uungu set up weekly check-ins to monitor progress and address any issues. "This is a marathon, not a sprint," he reminded the team. "We need to maintain consistent effort over the next few months to ensure our data is in top shape for migration."

As the Cloudacious discovery workshops progressed, Uungu made sure to keep the data team informed of any new requirements or insights that might affect their work.

"By the time we're ready to select our implementation partner," Uungu assured Zamba, "our data will be clean, deduplicated, and ready for migration. This upfront effort will save us significant time and resources during the implementation phase."

Despite the current state of their data, Uungu was optimistic.

With a robust data management strategy in place, he believed they could significantly improve data quality.

There was still a lot of work to be done, but Uungu felt confident that by the time implementation began, DataNova's data would be well-prepared for its transition to Salesforce.

Business Analysis and Requirements Specification

The analysis and requirements gathering phase is crucial for laying a solid foundation for any CRM implementation project.

Let me share some insights on three key elements that can ensure you have a clear understanding of your needs and a well-defined path forward.

Current and Future State Process Analysis

Understanding your current processes and envisioning future state workflows is essential for maximising the benefits of your new CRM system. It's not just about documenting what you do now – it's about imagining what you could do.

To effectively conduct process analysis:

- Involve stakeholders from all relevant departments in mapping current processes
- Encourage open discussion about pain points and inefficiencies in current workflows
- Demonstrate new system capabilities to spark ideas for process improvements
- Create visual representations of both current and desired future state processes
- Balance ambitious ideas with practical implementation considerations
- Identify quick wins that can deliver immediate value post-implementation

Failing to thoroughly analyse current and future state processes can lead to a CRM system that doesn't effectively support business needs, resulting in low user adoption and missed opportunities for efficiency gains.

Defining Clear Scope and Requirements

Clear, well-defined scope and requirements are critical for project success, managing expectations, and controlling costs. This is where the rubber meets the road – it's about translating all those workshop discussions and process maps into concrete, actionable items.

To effectively define project scope and requirements:

- Review and refine the requirements based on insights gained during discovery
- Prioritise requirements using a method like MoSCoW[16]
- Develop clear, measurable acceptance criteria for each requirement
- Create detailed requirements to capture specific functionality needs
- Involve key stakeholders in requirement review and validation
- Be prepared to justify the importance of each high-priority requirement

I've seen projects get into real trouble because of scope creep, where "nice-to-have" features are sneaked in as "must-haves."

It may be necessary to engage management consultants to help you to define your requirements if you do not have the internal capability to do so.

Neglecting to do this can result in budget overruns and a final solution that doesn't meet organisational needs.

Data Cleansing and Migration Planning

The Data cleansing workstream is one of the most neglected section of the project delivery because it's "boring". However, there are

---

[16] I prefer to have a priority rating of 1-5, where 1 is Must Have Right Now and 5 is Meh. It just makes it easier as we just work down the priority rating.

Discovery & Planning

ways to approach this important activity, such as using AI[17] to assist with more menial tasks of de-duplication[18].

Clean, well-structured data is critical for the success of any CRM system. Planning for data cleansing and migration early in the project is essential. In my experience, this is often the most underestimated part of a CRM implementation.

To effectively plan for data cleansing and migration:

- Assess the current state of data across all relevant sources
- Identify data quality issues such as duplicates, inconsistencies, and outdated information
- Develop a comprehensive data cleansing plan
- Create a data mapping strategy for migrating to the new system
- Assign resources and allocate time for data cleansing activities
- Develop a strategy for ongoing data quality maintenance

I had a client who insisted their data was "mostly clean." We ended up spending three additional months on data cleansing after go-live because of data quality issues.

Underestimating the importance of data quality can lead to a new CRM system filled with inaccurate or incomplete data, undermining its effectiveness and user trust.

In my experience, the most successful CRM implementations are those where the organisation took the time to really understand their needs, clearly define their requirements, and address data quality issues head-on.

It might feel like you're delaying the "real work" of implementation but trust me – this foundation will save you time, money, and headaches down the road.

---

[17] Be careful about the data privacy clauses of the LLM (Large Language Model) that is being used, as the data could be ingested and utilised for machine learning.
[18] Check out my other book Salesforce Discovery 101 – where I discuss other ways to approach the data cleansing workstream.

7
Design & Planning

Balancing current and future needs when designing your new system is an art form. Just make sure you don't let the glitter of shiny new things to supersede important considerations like security and performance.

Discovery & Planning

Uungu surveyed the conference room, where the Cloudacious team was setting up for another day of intense discussions. He knew the decisions made in the coming days would shape the entire CRM implementation.

As Coco, Cloudacious' Solution Architect, began her presentation on Salesforce's architecture, Uungu listened intently, jotting down key points.

"We need to decide how much we'll leverage out-of-the-box functionality versus custom development," Coco explained.

Amar, DataNova's CTO, voiced his concerns. "Custom development gives us exactly what we want, but could it be harder to maintain long-term?"

Coco nodded. "There's always a trade-off between customisation and long-term maintainability."

They debated each major design decision:

- *Data model: How closely to stick to Salesforce's standard objects?*
- *User interface: How much customisation was needed to match DataNova's processes?*
- *Integration: Which systems needed to connect with Salesforce, and how? Could this be scope for a future phase?*
- *Security model: How to balance data access with confidentiality requirements?*

Coco facilitated the workshops, but it was Uungu who mediated the discussions, pushing for clarity on each decision's implications.

"If we customise the opportunity object this much, how will it affect our ability to use standard Salesforce reports?" he asked at one point.

By day's end, they had a rough blueprint of their Salesforce design. Uungu felt both excited and cautious – they were creating something uniquely tailored to DataNova, but each customisation increased complexity.

* * *

The next morning, Uungu initiated a session on defining success metrics. "How will we know if this CRM implementation is successful?" he asked.

Azul, the Sales Director, replied, "We defined an expected ROI in the business case. Now we have to figure out how we are going to measure success. So in essence, we should see an increase in sales, right?"

"True," Uungu replied, "but we need to be more specific. How much of an increase? Over what time period?"

They brainstormed potential metrics:

- Sales metrics: Win rate, average deal size, sales cycle length
- Customer service metrics: Case resolution time, customer satisfaction scores
- Marketing metrics: Campaign ROI, lead conversion rates
- System adoption metrics: Login frequency, feature usage rates

Uungu encouraged the team to set concrete targets for each metric. "These KPIs will be how we judge the success of this entire project. We need to be ambitious but realistic."

* * *

As he was discussing metrics with his team, an email came in from Vi, Cloudacious' Project Manager.

"We need to review the RAIDD log and discuss the risks we're taking on."

Uungu replied to the email, "You're right. We should dedicate time to risk assessment and mitigation planning. Let's meet up before the end of the week."

Both project managers met and had a detailed session on risks detailing potential issues such as:

- Data migration issues
- User adoption challenges
- Integration complexities
- Performance concerns with heavy customisation
- Budget overruns

- Timeline delays

For each risk, they assessed the likelihood and potential impact, identifying specific mitigation strategies for high-priority risks.

"For user adoption," Uungu suggested, "we should plan hands-on training sessions and identify 'CRM champions' to support their colleagues."

As they worked through the risk register, both project managers felt a lot more confident. They weren't ignoring challenges but facing them head-on with concrete plans.

By week's end, Uungu looked at the conference room walls, now covered in diagrams, charts, and sticky notes. It represented hours of intense discussion, careful decision-making, and thoughtful planning.

He addressed his team, "Great work, everyone. We've got our blueprint, success metrics, and risk mitigation plans. It won't be easy, but I believe we're set up for success."

Design and Planning for Project Success

The design and planning phase is crucial for shaping the direction and outcomes of your CRM implementation.

Here are three key elements that I've found critical for success.

Making Design Decisions

Effective design decisions balance organisational needs with system capabilities, setting the foundation for a CRM that truly serves your business objectives.

To make effective design decisions:

- Evaluate the trade-offs between out-of-the-box functionality and custom development
- Consider long-term maintainability and scalability when choosing customisations
- Align your data model with both Salesforce standard objects and unique business requirements
- Design user interfaces that balance familiarity for users with process improvements
- Plan integrations carefully, considering data flow, security, and performance implications
- Develop a security model that protects sensitive data while ensuring necessary access

I had this one client who insisted on heavily customising standard objects. While it seemed to meet their immediate needs, it created significant challenges down the line when they wanted to upgrade or use new Salesforce features.

This created a mess of 'technical debt' that caused performance and functional issues in the system that needed a lot of re-work.

That's why it's crucial to think long-term when making design decisions.

Defining Success Metrics and KPIs

Clear, measurable success metrics and KPIs are essential for guiding the implementation and demonstrating the value of your CRM investment.

Use the list you created when crafting your business case, and continuously review and refine as the project progresses so you stay on track.

To effectively define success metrics and KPIs:

- Align metrics with overall business objectives
- Include a mix of quantitative and qualitative measures
- Set specific, time-bound targets for each metric
- Consider metrics across different areas: sales, customer service, marketing, and system adoption
- Ensure metrics are measurable within the new CRM system
- Plan for baseline measurements before implementation to enable before-and-after comparisons

I've seen projects where vague success criteria led to disagreements about whether the implementation was successful. Having clear, agreed-upon metrics from the start can prevent these issues and provide a shared vision of success.

Risk Assessment and Mitigation Planning

As with success metrics and KPIs detailed above, you should already have a risk register drafted when you created the business plan.

This should be a living document, and it needs to be constantly reviewed with your partner to make sure you always have your finger on the pulse of the project – and that as soon as you spot a risk materialising[19], you can immediately put mitigation action into practice.

---

[19] Risks that can't be mitigated will turn into Issues, which will need to be managed. These are also logged in the RAIDD log.

Proactive risk management is critical for navigating the complexities of CRM implementation and ensuring project success.

To conduct effective risk assessment and mitigation planning:

- Involve diverse stakeholders in identifying potential risks
- Assess both the likelihood and potential impact of each risk
- Prioritise risks based on their overall threat to project success
- Develop specific, actionable mitigation strategies for high-priority risks
- Assign ownership for each mitigation action
- Regularly review and update the risk register throughout the project
- Consider both technical risks (e.g., data migration issues) and organisational risks (e.g., user adoption challenges)

As a project manager for the consulting partner, I would always schedule a weekly meeting with the client to review all the items on the RAIDD log and the action log.[20]

We need to be proactive in managing our projects so that we can address potential issues before they become real problems and keep the project on track even if we might face complex challenges.

While it may be tempting to rush into implementation, taking the time for thorough design and planning is key to long-term CRM success.

I've seen rushed projects that seemed to save time initially, only to require extensive rework later.

Trust me - a solid foundation at this stage can save you countless hours and resources down the line.

---

[20] Before meeting with the client for project updates where we also go through the RAIDD log, I usually review it with key members of my team first.

8
Resourcing, Financing & Partnerships

Team members who are expected to work on the project on top of their day job will not be able to do either jobs well. Make sure you resource your project properly.

Discovery & Planning

Uungu studied the org chart on his screen, contemplating the resource needs for DataNova's CRM implementation. With the Cloudacious discovery phase concluding and CloudMasters' presentation imminent, it was time to solidify their internal resourcing strategy.

Zamba, the CEO, appeared at Uungu's door. "You look deep in thought. What's on your mind?"

Uungu invited her in. "I'm strategizing our resourcing for the implementation phase. We need a strong internal team without compromising our daily operations."

He outlined his hybrid team proposal:

- A full-time project manager (himself)
- A part-time business analyst, potentially seconded from a business unit
- A part-time technical lead from IT
- Full-time testing resources during User Acceptance Testing

"What about backfilling the roles for project team members?" Zamba inquired.

"I see this as an opportunity for junior staff development," Uungu explained. "We could also bring in temporary help if needed."

Zamba nodded approvingly. "It's good that you're considering both the project and DataNova's broader interest, Uungu."

The next day, Uungu found himself discussing finances with Hoong, the CFO.

"The estimated costs from Cloudacious are higher than anticipated," Hoong noted, "and we're still waiting on CloudMasters' proposal."

Uungu acknowledged this. "True, but remember, we expanded the scope during discovery. Let me walk you through my budget breakdown."

He presented a detailed spreadsheet categorising the cost:

- Software licensing and infrastructure
- Implementation partner fees
- Internal resource costs (including backfill for seconded employees)

- Training and change management
- Contingency fund

"I've included a 15% contingency," Uungu explained. "CRM implementations often uncover unexpected challenges."

Hoong raised an eyebrow. "15% seems high."

"It's insurance," Uungu countered. "If we don't use it, great. But if we need it, we won't have to request additional funds mid-project."

After a thorough review, Hoong agreed to support the budget at the next board meeting, with the caveat that he'd be monitoring costs closely.

As the final presentations approached, Uungu gathered his core team to discuss their vendor management strategy.

"Whichever partner we choose will be working closely with us for months," he reminded them. "We need to think beyond just technical capabilities."

They identified key criteria for evaluating partnerships:

- Communication style and frequency
- Approach to knowledge transfer
- Flexibility and adaptability
- Cultural fit with DataNova
- Long-term support and partnership potential

Azul emphasised, "It's not just about the implementation. We need a partner who can support our future growth."

Uungu agreed, outlining his ideas for collaboration:

- Regular status meetings with clear agendas and action items
- A shared project management tool for transparency
- Designated points of contact on both sides
- Clear escalation paths for issues
- Joint problem-solving sessions for complex challenges

"Most importantly," Uungu added, "we need to view them as partners, not just vendors. Their success is our success."

Discovery & Planning

As the meeting concluded, Uungu felt a sense of readiness. With a solid resourcing plan, a carefully managed budget, and a clear vision for vendor partnership, they were well-positioned for the CRM implementation journey ahead.

Capacity Building, Capital and Collaborations

Effective resource management and strong partnerships are critical to project success. Start planning right at the beginning of the project, and don't wait until the implementation is almost complete before asking questions about the resourcing!

Here are three key elements that I've seen make a significant difference.

Resourcing the Project Team

Assembling the right team with the right skills is crucial for a successful CRM project – both during the project implementation as well as after go-live. It requires balancing project needs with ongoing operational requirements.

To effectively resource your project team:

- Identify key roles needed for the project, including both full-time and part-time positions
- Consider a hybrid team structure, blending dedicated project resources with subject matter experts from business units
- Plan for backfilling roles of team members seconded to the project, or reducing the workload or commitment of the project team members for the duration of the project
- Use the project as an opportunity for employee development and growth
- Ensure a mix of technical skills, business knowledge, and soft skills in your team
- Plan for resource needs across different project phases, from implementation to post-go-live support

I've seen so many projects where the client had not sufficiently resourced their project team – expecting people to dedicate time on the project as well as doing their day job.

The result was constant conflicts between project work and their daily responsibilities, leading to delays and frustration.

This is not fair, and I've seen people burn out trying to juggle everything that is on their plate.

A balanced approach, like Uungu's hybrid team, often yields better results.

Budget Planning and Cost Management

Careful financial planning and management are essential to keep your CRM project on track and demonstrate ROI.

To effectively plan and manage your project budget:

- Develop a comprehensive budget covering all aspects of the project
- Benchmark costs against industry standards to ensure reasonableness
- Build in a contingency fund to cover unexpected expenses or challenges[21]
- Break down costs by project phase and track spending against budgeted amounts
- Regularly review and update the budget as the project progresses
- Be prepared to justify major expenses to stakeholders and decision-makers
- Consider both short-term implementation costs and long-term operational costs

Projects can be derailed by unexpected costs that weren't budgeted for.

Uungu's approach of including a substantial contingency fund is a good idea. It's always better to have a buffer and not need it, than to need it and not have it.[22]

---

[21] I cannot overstate how important this is. You don't know what you don't know until you know it.
[22] How much contingency to put aside will depend on the risks and complexity of the project.

Partner Management and Collaboration Strategies

Your implementation partner plays a crucial role in your project's success. Effective partner management and collaboration are key to a productive, long-term partnership.

To manage vendor relationships effectively:

- Develop clear criteria for evaluating potential implementation partners, beyond just technical capabilities
- Establish clear communication protocols, including regular status meetings and designated points of contact
- Implement shared project management tools for transparency and collaboration
- Create clear escalation paths for issue resolution
- Foster a partnership mentality rather than an us-them relationship
- Plan for knowledge transfer to build internal capabilities
- Align success metrics and regularly review progress together
- Consider long-term support and partnership potential when selecting a vendor

As the project manager for the consulting partner, I usually try to encourage a relationship where the client would treat us as an extension of their team, as we would be involved in strategic discussions and problem-solving sessions.

There would not be an "us" and a "them" situation. There would only be an "all of us as a project team" which consist of people from both partner and client side, and it would be up to us as a team to bring the project home.

Effective resource management and partnership are ongoing processes that require continuous attention throughout the project lifecycle.

Regularly reassessing your team composition, monitoring your budget, and nurturing your relationship with your partner will help you navigate challenges and capitalise on opportunities as your CRM implementation progresses.

Discovery & Planning

9
Evaluating Deliverables and Vendor Proposals

Evaluate partner proposals and their deliverables carefully. For example: poorly written documents are a sign of poor governance and should raise scrutiny.

Uungu stood at the head of the conference table, surveying the stacks of documents before him. These were the culmination of weeks of discovery work from both Cloudacious and CloudMasters.

"Alright, team," Uungu began, his voice steady. "You've all had an opportunity to review the deliverables and add your comments. Let's go through it all in detail."

"Let's start with the current state analysis provided by Cloudacious. Azul, I see you've made a comment about their assessment of our sales process. Do you want to expand on that?"

Azul leaned forward, brow furrowed. "They've captured most of it accurately, but I think they've underestimated the complexity of our proposal process. It's not just a simple approval workflow."

Uungu nodded, making a note. "Good catch. We'll need to clarify that with them."

They methodically reviewed all the comments from every stakeholder within each deliverable such as:

- *Process maps*
- *System landscape diagrams*
- *Data models*
- *User stories*
- *Implementation roadmaps*
- *Risk assessments*

For each item, Uungu encouraged frank discussion, pushing the team to critically evaluate the quality and completeness of the deliverables from both vendors.

When they reached CloudMasters' proposed data migration strategy, Amar, the CTO, raised a concern. "Their timeline seems overly optimistic. Given the state of our data, I think we're looking at least an extra two weeks for cleansing and validation."

Uungu appreciated Amar's insight. "Excellent point. Let's flag that for further discussion."

By the end of the day, they had a comprehensive assessment of both vendors' deliverables, complete with a list of follow-up questions and areas needing clarification.

Discovery & Planning

* * *

The following week, Uungu prepared for the final presentations from both vendors. As Cloudacious began their presentation, he felt a mix of fatigue and anticipation.

Clem, Cloudacious' lead Business Analyst, began with energy. "We've identified several opportunities for improvement in DataNova's processes," she explained, outlining their findings and proposed solutions.

Coco, the Solution Architect, followed with their technical approach. "We believe a custom AppExchange package combined with tailored automation will significantly streamline your sales process," she explained, her expertise evident.

Vi, the Project Manager, concluded with a detailed project plan, emphasising their risk mitigation strategies and feedback loops. She also walked through the commercial proposal for their complete implementation of the Salesforce solution.

As the Cloudacious team fielded questions, Uungu noted how well they interacted with the DataNova stakeholders.

There was a synergy that resonated with DataNova's collaborative culture.

* * *

After both presentations were complete, Uungu gathered his evaluation committee. "Now comes the challenge of making a decision. Let's review our scoring matrix."

They went through their comprehensive scoring matrix with weighted criteria:

- *Technical Solution (30%)*
- *Project Approach (25%)*
- *Team Expertise (20%)*
- *Cultural Fit (15%)*
- *Cost (10%)*

"Remember," Uungu reminded the team, "we're looking for value, not just the lowest price."

As they began scoring, Uungu ensured input from various departments. Amar praised Cloudacious' technical approach, while Hoong appreciated their phased implementation plan. Azul was impressed with their understanding of DataNova's sales processes.

As the discussion progressed, Uungu noticed a recurring theme around cultural fit. "The Cloudacious team seemed to gel well with ours," he observed.

Zamba, who had been listening quietly, agreed. "There was a certain synergy in their interactions with us."

They added cultural fit questions to their matrix and completed the scoring. While both vendors had strong technical capabilities, Cloudacious had an edge in project approach and cultural fit.

"Unless there are any objections," Uungu said, reviewing the final scores, "it seems we have our implementation partner."

The room buzzed with anticipation. They all recognised the transformative journey ahead for DataNova.

Uungu felt a sense of accomplishment. Their thorough discovery process, careful evaluation of deliverables, and thoughtful vendor assessment had led to a decision that felt right on multiple levels.

As he prepared to draft the decision document for Zamba's approval, he realised that selecting a Salesforce partner was more than just a technical decision – it was about finding the right fit for DataNova's future.

Discovery & Planning

The Beauty Pageant: Evaluating Vendor Proposals

It is important to thoroughly evaluate both discovery deliverables and vendor proposals to set up for project success.

Let's talk about the three key strategies I've seen make a significant difference.

Evaluating Discovery Deliverables

Thorough evaluation of discovery deliverables ensures that the groundwork laid during the discovery phase accurately reflects your organisation's needs and sets the right direction for implementation.

To effectively evaluate discovery deliverables:

- Assemble a cross-functional team to review deliverables, ensuring diverse perspectives[23]
- Create a structured evaluation framework with clear criteria for each type of deliverable
- Compare deliverables against the original project objectives and requirements
- Assess the quality, completeness, and accuracy of each deliverable
- Encourage critical thinking and challenge assumptions where necessary
- Identify gaps or areas needing clarification and create a plan to address them

Projects where the deliverable review process is rushed often leads to significant misunderstandings during implementation, resulting in costly rework.

---

[23] One of the challenges of inviting people who were not involved in discovery and design to review the deliverables is that you might end up having to manage scope discussions and having to justify and explain every design decision that were made, so proceed with caution!

The partners are likely to have a deliverable acceptance procedure where you'll have set time to comment and review the deliverables.

However, it is important to evaluate the deliverables thoroughly because it can save substantial time and frustration down the line.

Use a Standardised Scoring System

A well-designed scoring system provides a structured approach to comparing vendor proposals objectively and ensures that all critical factors are considered.

To effectively create a standardised scoring system:

- Identify key evaluation criteria based on your project requirements
- Assign weights to each criterion based on its importance to your project
- Develop a scoring scale (e.g., 1-4 or 1-8) for each criterion
- Create a scoring matrix or spreadsheet to calculate weighted scores
- Include both quantitative and qualitative measures in your scoring system

When project decisions are made based on 'gut feelings' rather than objective criteria, it often leads to challenges during implementation when expectations don't align with reality.

A standardised scoring system helps avoid such pitfalls[24].

Consider Cultural Fit and Technical Capabilities

While technical capabilities are crucial, the cultural alignment between your organisation and the vendor can significantly impact the success of your CRM implementation.

---

[24] Check out the Appendix for a copy of the Vendor Matrix

To effectively evaluate cultural fit:

- Assess the vendor's communication style and responsiveness during the discovery process
- Evaluate how well the vendor's team collaborates with your staff
- Consider the vendor's values and how they align with your organisation's values
- Assess the vendor's approach to problem-solving and conflict resolution
- Include questions about work style and company culture in your reference checks

Evaluating deliverables and vendor proposals is not just about ticking boxes or finding the cheapest option. It's about ensuring you have a solid foundation for your project and identifying a partner who can work effectively with you and your team through the trials and tribulations of implementing change and initiatives.

They need to be able to understand your unique needs and contribute to the long-term success of your CRM initiative. Taking the time to thoroughly address these elements can make the difference between a challenging implementation and a transformative success.

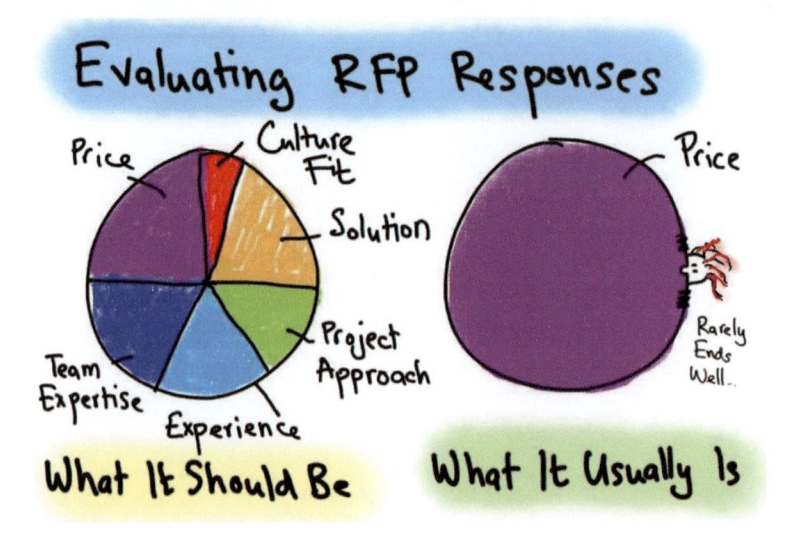

Evaluating RFP Responses

What It Should Be — pie chart with segments: Price, Culture Fit, Solution, Project Approach, Experience, Team Expertise

What It Usually Is — pie chart entirely Price (Rarely Ends Well)

10
From Discovery to Implementation

The real benefit of a discovery phase is risk mitigation, and structured transition to project implementation will set the project up for success.

Uungu stood at the whiteboard, a sense of accomplishment visible as he drew a checkmark next to "Select Implementation Partner." Cloudacious had won the bid, their thorough discovery and compelling presentation sealing the deal.

Vi, the Project Manager from Cloudacious, waved at the DataNova team on the video call. "Thank you so much for selecting Cloudacious as your partner of choice. Now that we have completed discovery, I would like to walk through the draft transition plan I prepared. Is that ok?"

Uungu nodded, and Vi shared her screen, revealing a detailed timeline.

"The key," Vi explained, "is to have a smooth handover from the discovery team to the implementation team. We usually try to keep the same team for discovery and implementation – however, it is not possible at this time because Clem our business analyst will be leaving for a sabbatical. She will be replaced by Tangerine, a consultant who is just as qualified and experienced."

Uungu liked the idea but had concerns. "How do we ensure we don't lose critical knowledge in the handover?"

Vi had anticipated this. "We'll have comprehensive knowledge transfer sessions before Clem leaves so that Tangerine will be up to speed. We are also keeping Coco, our Solution Architect, on for the initial implementation phase."

Hoong, the CFO, raised a critical point. "What about our own internal readiness? How do we ensure our team is prepared for the implementation phase?"

Uungu had been thinking about this. "I propose we run a series of internal calls in the week leading up to the transition and the implementation project kick-off. We'll cover project objectives, expected changes, and individual roles and responsibilities."

He continued, "We'll also need to ensure all stakeholders are aligned on the project goals and their part in achieving them. This includes setting clear expectations for time commitments and decision-making processes."

As the meeting wound down, Zamba spoke up. "Uungu, how will we know we're truly ready to begin implementation?"

Uungu appreciated the challenge. "I propose we create a comprehensive readiness checklist. It would cover things like:

- *All discovery deliverables approved and signed off*
- *Implementation team fully staffed and onboarded*
- *Internal stakeholders briefed and prepared*
- *Project charter and scope finalised and approved*
- *Initial risk mitigation strategies in place*
- *Budget and resources secured for the first implementation phase*

We don't move forward until every item on that list is checked off."

Uungu added, "Importantly, we need to ensure our project scope is clearly defined and understood by all parties. Any ambiguities or potential scope creep should be addressed now, before we start implementation."

Zamba nodded, satisfied with the answer. "Excellent. That gives me confidence we're not rushing into implementation unprepared."

As the meeting adjourned, Uungu felt a mix of excitement and nervousness. They were on the cusp of moving from planning to action, from theory to practice.

Later that evening, as Uungu updated the project timeline, he paused to reflect. They had come so far already, but the journey was really just beginning. He glanced at a small mirror on his desk, seeing determination in his eyes and a hint of a smile beneath his purple goatee.

"Ready or not," he muttered to himself, "here we go."

Transitioning From Discovery to Implementation

Transition is an activity that is commonly ignored, and poor handover process can result in important things slipping through the cracks.

Knowledge Transfer and Team Continuity

Ensuring a smooth transfer of knowledge from the discovery team to the implementation team is crucial. I've seen projects falter when key insights from discovery were lost in the transition.

To effectively manage knowledge transfer:

- Plan detailed handover sessions between discovery and implementation teams
- Create comprehensive documentation of discovery findings and decisions
- Maintain continuity by keeping key personnel consistent across phases
- Use collaborative tools to capture and share knowledge throughout the project

I once worked on a project where we failed to properly document the rationale behind certain design decisions made during discovery. This led to confusion and rework during implementation. Since then, I've always emphasised the importance of thorough knowledge transfer.

Internal Readiness and Stakeholder Alignment

Preparing your organisation for the implementation phase is as important as the technical preparations. I've seen technically sound projects struggle due to lack of internal readiness.

To ensure internal readiness:

- Conduct sessions to brief stakeholders on project objectives and their roles
- Clearly communicate expected changes and impacts on day-to-day operations
- Establish clear decision-making processes and escalation paths
- Assess and address any skills gaps in the internal team

I recall a project where we overlooked preparing the sales team for the upcoming changes and their resistance during implementation caused significant delays.

What had happened was that their office configuration was being changed from open plan to separated cubicles, which was a highly unpopular move. While this was not the main reason for the resistance, it was a contributory factor.

Sometimes too much change can be difficult for people to cope – which is why it should be managed properly.

Project Scope and Readiness Checklist

A clear project scope and a comprehensive readiness checklist are your safeguards against a premature or ill-prepared start to implementation.

To ensure project readiness:

- Develop a detailed readiness checklist covering all aspects of the project
- Clearly define and document the project scope, including what's out of scope
- Establish a formal sign-off process for the transition to implementation

The transition from discovery to implementation is not just a handover of documents. It's a critical phase where the strategic work of discovery transforms into the practical efforts of implementation.

By focusing on knowledge transfer, internal readiness, and project scope, you create a solid bridge between these phases, setting your project up for success.

Discovery & Planning

Approach this transition with diligence and attention to detail. It may feel like you're delaying the real work, but trust me, the time invested here will pay dividends throughout the implementation phase and beyond. It's your best chance to ensure that the promises of discovery become reality in implementation.

Donuts for project kick-off is optional but highly recommended!

Project implementation

Project implementation

11
The Build part of the project

Emotional Cycle of Change (ECOC): Keep your eye on the project during build phase, as it's when the Valley of Despair sentiment is likely to hit. Monitor and manage it closely to turn this around into a success.

Vi, the Project Manager from Cloudacious, stood at the front of the room, and connected her laptop to the projector.

With a few clicks, she brought up a detailed timeline on the large screen, revealing a series of two-week iterations stretching out before them.

"Now that we've moved into the build phase," Vi explained, "We'll be working in these short iterations to deliver incremental value. This approach will allow us to build the requirements in chunks and show you our progress as we build out the Salesforce system."

Uungu nodded, appreciating the structured approach.

He did have a question though, "How do we ensure we're staying on track with each iteration? Two weeks seems like a short time to make meaningful progress."

Vi smiled, having anticipated this question.

"Thank you for that question, Uungu. We have a robust process in place that help us do that and keeps us aligned."

She began outlining their approach, "The project team will have daily stand-ups to address any immediate concerns or blockers. These are short calls in the mornings – lasting no more than 15 minutes where we provide a quick update of what we've done, what we are planning to do that day, and whether we are blocked (and who can help unblock our work).

"And then, at the end of these two-week iterations, we'll hold show and tell sessions to demonstrate the features we've built. That way you can see our progress which helps you visualise what your system will look like at the end of the project.

"And finally, at the end of each iteration, we'll conduct a session called a 'retrospective' which allows us to continuously improve our process. It is a review of what went well, and what could have been improved."

* * *

As the weeks progressed, Uungu found himself immersed in a whirlwind of activities, each playing a crucial role in bringing their Salesforce vision to life.

Every two weeks, Uungu would sit in the iteration planning session together with key team members and the Cloudacious team where they would review the product backlog[25] in detail.

These sessions were intense but productive, as they prioritised user stories and set clear goals for the upcoming sprint.

Uungu particularly enjoyed these meetings, as they gave him a tangible sense of progress and allowed him to steer the project towards DataNova's most pressing needs.

"For this iteration," Uungu said during one such meeting, "I think we should prioritise the custom dashboard for our sales reps. They've been asking for better visibility into their pipeline."

Kijani nodded in agreement. "Absolutely. That would be a game-changer for my team."

The daily stand-ups quickly became a cornerstone of Uungu's routine. Each morning, he would join a brief check-in with the Cloudacious team. These quick meetings were invaluable for addressing any blockers promptly and ensuring the project maintained its momentum.

During one stand-up, Amar raised a concern. "We're having some issues with the data migration script. It's not handling some of our legacy data formats correctly."

Uungu appreciated the early flag. "Thanks for bringing that up, Amar. Vi, can we get one of your data specialists to look at this today?"

Vi nodded. "Absolutely. I'll have Aqua message you right after this meeting, Amar."

The show and tell sessions at the end of each iteration were always a highlight. Uungu watched with growing pride as Cloudacious demonstrated the features they had built, bringing their CRM vision to life piece by piece.

---

[25] A product backlog is a list of requirements in the form of user stories. See Appendix for Glossary.

The iteration retrospectives provided a valuable opportunity for reflection and improvement and Uungu would participate in these sessions along with the Cloudacious project team.

"I noticed we had some delays getting feedback on the page layouts," Uungu pointed out during one retro. "How can we streamline that process?"

This led to a productive discussion and improved workflow for the next iteration, with dedicated time slots for layout reviews built into their schedule.

Throughout the build process, Uungu found himself frequently pulled into smaller design sessions.

These focused meetings allowed the Cloudacious team to clarify requirements or discuss complex functionality. Uungu relished these deep dives, as they often led to innovative solutions that perfectly fit DataNova's unique needs.

As the Salesforce system began taking shape, Uungu realised that staying on top of the build process required constant vigilance.

He focused on three key areas to ensure the project's success.

First was active engagement and rapid feedback between the project team members.

Vi had set up a dedicated Slack channel for real-time communication between DataNova and Cloudacious. Uungu made it his mission to foster a culture of quick responses within his team.

"Remember," he told his team during a check-in, "in this phase, time is of the essence. Let's aim to respond to queries within hours, not days. It keeps the momentum going and prevents bottlenecks."

The second focus area was balancing current needs with future scalability. "How will this solution scale as we grow?" became Uungu's mantra during design sessions.

He constantly challenged the team to think beyond immediate requirements, ensuring that today's solutions wouldn't become tomorrow's limitations.

Project implementation

During one design session, when discussing the structure of customer records, Uungu raised a crucial point. "We're expanding into new markets next year. How can we design this to accommodate different business structures we might encounter?"

This forward-thinking approach led to a more flexible design that would serve DataNova well into the future.

The third key area was maintaining continuous alignment with business objectives.

At every show and tell, Uungu made a point of reminding the team of DataNova's core objectives for the CRM implementation. This consistent focus helped ensure that every feature and decision supported their overall goals.

* * *

As the build phase progressed, Uungu could see the progress of their Salesforce system.

It was taking shape beautifully, and was evolving from abstract concepts into a tangible tool that would transform DataNova's operations.

However, he knew that the real test was yet to come.

User Acceptance Testing loomed on the horizon, and with it, the moment of truth when DataNova's team would get their hands on the system for the first time.

Client Involvement in the CRM Build Phase

I've found that active client involvement during the build phase is crucial for project success. Here are three crucial key areas.

Consistent and Timely Communication

Effective communication is the cornerstone of successful client involvement during the build phase. To ensure clear and timely communication:

- Establish dedicated communication channels (e.g., Slack, Microsoft Teams) for quick queries and updates
- Set expectations for response times to developer questions
- Participate actively in daily stand-ups to stay informed of progress and address issues promptly
- Ensure key stakeholders attend all show & tell sessions to provide immediate feedback

When working with a consulting partner, it pays to remember that time is money so the quicker issues can be resolved, the less likely the project will end up with a budget over-run.

Meaningful and Actionable Feedback

The quality of feedback provided during the build phase significantly impacts the final CRM system. To provide effective feedback:

- Come prepared to show & tell sessions with a clear understanding of what to expect
- Offer specific, constructive feedback rather than vague comments
- Prioritise feedback based on business impact and implementation complexity
- Be open to alternative solutions proposed by the implementation team

- Validate that feedback aligns with overall project goals before requesting changes

Vague feedback usually leads to multiple rounds of revisions and frustration on both sides which is why I always advocate for structured feedback processes that align with project goals.

Align Implementation with Business Objectives

Keeping the project aligned with core business objectives ensures the CRM delivers real value. To maintain alignment:

- Create a simple scorecard mapping features to key business objectives
- Review this scorecard regularly during the build phase
- Ensure all major design decisions support at least one core business objective
- Be prepared to justify any custom development in terms of business value

Your active involvement during the build phase is not just about overseeing the technical implementation.

It's about ensuring that the final CRM system truly serves your organisation's needs and sets the stage for successful adoption and utilisation.

Approach this phase as a collaborative journey with your implementation partner, and you'll be well on your way to CRM success.

Project implementation

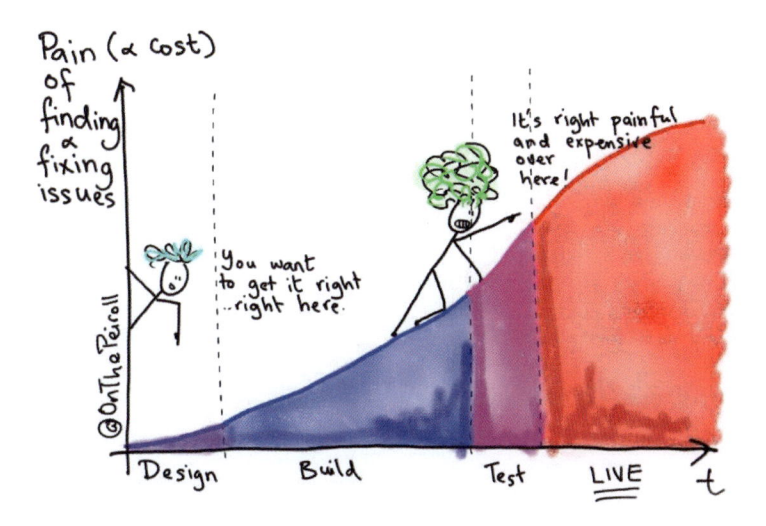

The Rule of Ten says: "the cost and effort required to fix a problem or implement a change increases exponentially as a project progresses" Essentially: The longer you wait, the pain-ier it gets.

12
Planning for Quality

Quality Assurance is about asking the right questions.

Uungu stood at the whiteboard, his expression a mix of determination and anticipation as he wrote "QA and User Acceptance Testing" at the top.

"Team," he addressed the assembled group, "The project is still in the build phase, but we need to prepare to test and put our CRM through its paces and ensure it meets all our needs."

Uungu's first task was to assemble a testing team from across DataNova. He turned to Azul, the Sales Director. "I need your top performers who know the sales process inside and out."

Azul nodded, already considering her candidates.

"Amar," Uungu continued, "we'll need the support of your IT department to help with the testing too."

With the team assembled, Uungu collaborated with Vi from Cloudacious to conduct a series of training workshops so that the test team understood the features that were out of the box versus the new functionalities that were being configured and developed for DataNova.

Vi emphasised the importance of their role: "Your job is to find defects – i.e. issues that highlight where we have not built the system to specification.

"By the time you get your hands on the system during UAT, we at Cloudacious will already have completed our own testing that covers process flow testing, also called systems testing, as well as integration and data migration testing.

"Your role is to make sure that what we've built supports your business workflows effectively. It may be that you will discover additional features that were missed out when we did discovery – and if so, we'll be able to discuss this change and its priority and its impact within the timeline of this project. And then we can make a decision about it."

"Actually," Uungu paused. "We need to make sure that our system will support our business processes with our leads and our customers. There are likely to be real life scenarios that we have missed when designing our system, so we'll have to decide how to handle it – for example whether we find a manual workaround or document it as a future requirement."

***

Next, Uungu turned his focus on creating a comprehensive test plan.vHe worked closely with Coco, the Solution Architect from Cloudacious, to define the objectives and scope of the UAT.

"You need to cover every critical business process," Coco said. "From lead generation to closed deals, from campaign management to customer service."

They spent several days refining the test plan, establishing timelines, and allocating resources.

Uungu emphasised the need for clear pass/fail criteria for each test case to enable data-driven decisions about go-live readiness.

As the test cases accumulated, Uungu realised they needed realistic test data. He collaborated with Amar to create a sanitised copy of their production data for testing.

"This way," Uungu explained, "we're testing with data that reflects our actual business complexity, without risking sensitive information."

The day before UAT was set to begin, Uungu gathered the team for a final briefing. Looking around the room, he saw a mix of excitement and focus on their faces.

"Tomorrow, we will start putting our new CRM through its paces," he said. "This isn't just about finding bugs. It's about ensuring this system will truly support and enhance our business processes. Each of you brings unique expertise to this process. Trust your knowledge, be thorough, and speak up if something doesn't feel right."

As the meeting concluded, Uungu felt the familiar tension of a project reaching its critical phase. The UAT would be intense, but he knew it was necessary to refine and validate their CRM implementation.

Uungu allowed himself a small smile. They were well-prepared, and he had confidence in his team. Whatever challenges the UAT phase might bring, he knew that DataNova was ready to face them head-on.

The quality quest was about to begin, and Uungu was eager to see their CRM vision put to the test.

Planning for User Acceptance Testing

In my years of experience with CRM implementations, I've found that User Acceptance Testing (UAT) is a critical phase that can make or break a project.

Here are three key areas that deserve special attention:

Select and Train the Right UAT Team

The success of UAT largely depends on having the right people involved and adequately prepared.

To effectively select and train your UAT team:

- Identify key users from various departments who understand business processes deeply
- Include a mix of power users and average users to get diverse perspectives
- Review the requirements with the UAT team so that they are aware of what has been built during project implementation
- Provide comprehensive training on base product as well as the new functionality
- Ensure testers understand the importance of critical thinking and attention to detail
- Foster a "tester mindset" that promotes curiosity, encourages exploratory testing, and focuses on uncovering edge cases.

In a project where we rushed through tester selection and training, the testing ended up being superficial, overlooking critical issues that surfaced after go-live. This experience underscores the need for thorough tester preparation.

Develop a Comprehensive Test Plan

A well-structured test plan provides a roadmap for the entire UAT process. To create an effective test plan:

- Clearly define test objectives aligned with project goals and success criteria
- Establish a realistic timeline that allows for thorough testing without rushing
- Allocate adequate resources, including personnel, environments, and tools
- Define clear pass/fail criteria for test cases to enable objective evaluation
- Develop detailed test scripts that cover all critical business scenarios
- Include plans for retesting and regression testing after fixes are implemented
- Consider non-functional requirements such as performance, usability, and security – especially if these are part of the signed-off requirements

When you underestimate the time needed for thorough testing, you are likely to rush the UAT phase. This could result in missed critical scenarios and difficulty in determining whether your CRM Is truly ready for go-live.

Prepare Realistic Test Data

Using representative test data is crucial for validating that the CRM will work with real-world information.

To prepare effective test data:

- Use a sanitised copy of production data when possible, to reflect true data complexity
- Ensure test data covers a wide range of scenarios and edge cases
- Include both valid and invalid data to test system behaviour and validations
- Prepare sufficient volume of data to test system performance under realistic loads

- Ensure test data aligns with the scenarios outlined in your test scripts

Your investment in thorough UAT preparation will pay dividends in the form of a higher quality CRM system, increased user satisfaction, and a smoother transition to the new system.

13
User Acceptance Testing (UAT)

Murphy's Law of QA: The more bugs you squash in planning, the fewer will sneak into UAT.

As the CRM implementation progressed, Uungu knew they were approaching a critical juncture: User Acceptance Testing (UAT). He gathered his core team in the conference room, determination evident in his expression.

"Team," Uungu began, "we're entering the UAT phase. This is our chance to ensure the CRM truly meets our needs before we go live."

"We need to focus on three key areas: distinguishing between defects and change requests, effectively logging and triaging issues, and ensuring a smooth UAT process."

He turned to the whiteboard and wrote "Defects vs. Change Requests."

"First," Uungu said, "we need to be clear on what constitutes a defect versus a change request. Kijani, any thoughts?"

"A defect is when the system doesn't work as specified in our requirements. A change request is asking for new or different functionality."

"Exactly," Uungu agreed. "Here's a question: Kijani, imagine you're testing the lead assignment feature, and you notice it's not factoring in the lead's industry. Is this a defect or a change request?"

Kijani thought for a moment. "Well, if our original requirements specified that lead assignment should consider industry, it's a defect. If we didn't include that in our requirements, it would be a change request."

"Perfect," Uungu smiled. "This distinction is crucial. It impacts how we prioritise and address issues during UAT."

Next, Uungu wrote "Logging and Triaging Issues" on the whiteboard.

"We need a robust process for logging and prioritising the issues we find," he explained. "Jade, any suggestions?"

Merah, an intern from IT put her hand up and answered for Jade, "We could use a ticketing system. Each issue should include steps to reproduce, expected vs. actual results, and screenshots if applicable."

"Great idea," Uungu nodded. "And for triage, we'll need a daily meeting at the end of the day to review new issues and prioritise them based on severity and impact."

Project implementation

The team spent the next hour detailing their issue management process, ensuring everyone understood their role.

Finally, Uungu wrote "Smooth UAT Process" on the board.

"Running a smooth UAT is critical," he said. "We need to ensure our testers are well-prepared and supported throughout the process."

Azul chimed in, "We should provide comprehensive training to our UAT team before we start. Maybe create detailed test scripts for each of our test cases to guide them?"

"Absolutely," Uungu agreed. "We'll also need to set up a 'war room' where testers can get immediate support if they encounter issues."

The team collaborated on creating a UAT plan, including a schedule, resource allocation, and communication strategies.

As the meeting wound down, Uungu looked at his team with pride. "Remember, UAT is not just about finding problems. It's our opportunity to ensure this CRM truly works for DataNova. Let's make the most of it."

* * *

The next week, as UAT kicked off, Uungu stood in the newly established war room, watching as testers diligently worked through their scripts. He overheard a conversation between two sales reps:

"Hey, the system isn't automatically sending follow-up emails after meetings. Is that a defect?" one asked.

The other rep checked the requirements document. "No, that wasn't in the original scope. Let's log it as a change request for future enhancement."

Uungu smiled to himself. His team was applying what they had learned, distinguishing between defects and change requests effectively.

Later that day, during the triage meeting, Uungu watched as Amar led the team through the day's logged issues.

"We have a high-priority defect in the pipeline dashboard," Amar reported. "Several testers have confirmed it. I suggest we escalate this to the development team at Cloudacious immediately."

As the UAT phase progressed, Uungu's careful planning paid off. The war room buzzed with activity, but there was an underlying sense of order and purpose. Testers felt supported, issues were being addressed promptly, and the CRM was steadily improving.

By the end of UAT, Uungu stood before his team. "Great work, everyone. Thanks to your diligence and attention to detail, we've not only identified and resolved critical issues but also compiled a valuable list of future enhancements. We're now one step closer to a CRM system that truly serves DataNova's needs."

As the team celebrated their successful UAT phase, Uungu allowed himself a moment of quiet pride.

They had navigated the tough emotional roller coaster of user acceptance, emerging with a stronger, more refined CRM system. The journey wasn't over, but this critical milestone filled him with confidence for the road ahead.

User Acceptance Testing in CRM Implementation

User Acceptance Testing (UAT) is such a critical phase that can often make or break a project.

Defects and Change Requests

Clearly differentiating between defects and change requests is crucial for effective UAT and project management.

To effectively distinguish between defects and change requests:

- Clearly define what constitutes a defect versus a change request at the outset of UAT
- Train your UAT team to recognise the difference
- Create a decision tree or flowchart to guide testers in categorising and logging issues
- Regularly review categorisations as a team to ensure consistency
- Establish a process for converting legitimate change requests into future enhancements
- Document all decisions for future reference and continuous improvement

Projects that lack clear distinction between defect and change usually leads to a high 'bug' count, which can cause unnecessary panic and can derail the project timeline.[26]

That's why it's really important to outline this distinction in UAT planning and execution.

---

[26] I usually have "Training" as an additional category for UAT issues because sometimes logged issues reflect the fact that the tester was unfamiliar about out-of-the-box features of the system, and may indicate more detailed training might be needed to increase user adoption.

Robust Issue Logging and Triage Processes

Effective issue management is essential for addressing problems efficiently and maintaining project momentum during UAT.

To implement effective issue logging and triage:

- Use a dedicated issue tracking system accessible to all testers and stakeholders[27]
- Create clear guidelines for logging issues, including necessary details and reproducibility steps
- Establish a severity and priority matrix to help in issue categorisation
- Conduct daily triage meetings to review and prioritise new issues
- Assign clear ownership for issue resolution and follow-up
- Maintain transparent communication about issue status and resolution timelines

Poor issue management can lead to issues or defects being reported multiple times, which could lead to overlooking critical defects and result in frustrated testers.

Ensure a Smooth and Efficient UAT Process

A well-organised UAT process not only identifies issues effectively but also builds user confidence in the new system.

To run a smooth and efficient UAT:

- Involve end-users from various roles to ensure comprehensive coverage
- Empower end-users to take ownership of their processes
- Encourage feedback on what other new features might be useful to drive business value
- Make sure everyone understands the issue management process so that all are clear about how issues are reported, triaged and managed

---

[27] Sometimes a simple spreadsheet will do, but you can also get really sophisticated with defect tracking tools like JIRA or Microsoft DevOps.

- Provide comprehensive training to UAT participants before testing begins on how to log issues such as the steps used to reproduce the issue alongside any screenshots and error codes
- Set up a dedicated "war room" or support channel for immediate assistance during testing
- Establish clear entry and exit criteria for the UAT phase
- Regularly communicate progress, including metrics on issues found and resolved
- Celebrate successes and recognise participant contributions throughout the process

UAT is more than just a technical exercise; it's an opportunity for users to gain confidence in the new system and for the project team to validate that the CRM truly meets business needs.

I believe that the UAT phase is a chance to generate buzz by making the project engaging and fun, since this is when users get their first hands-on experience with the new system.

I've seen projects achieve amazing success when the team approached UAT playfully — using creative, internal communications and making testing an exciting phase of the project. This approach helped generate enthusiasm and engagement across the user base.

Equally important is the "Go/No-Go" meeting at the end of UAT, where the team assesses if UAT has been successful.

This crucial decision point evaluates whether testing has verified the system as ready for go-live. If significant issues remain — whether unresolved defects, critical change requests, or missed requirements — the team may decide not to proceed. Yet.

Ensuring that the system meets the required standards and addresses essential business needs here is vital for a smooth go-live and for building user confidence.

By approaching UAT with the same rigor and strategic focus as other critical business processes, you not only ensure that users are well-prepared but also position the project for successful adoption.

14
Change Management & User Adoption

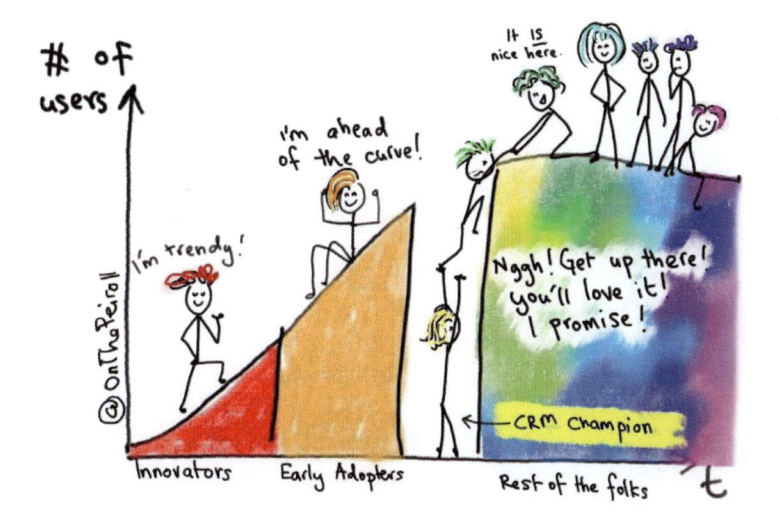

CRM champions are crucial in helping increase user adoption by helping people cross "The Chasm" (see "Crossing the Chasm" by Geoffrey Moore)

Project implementation

Uungu stood before the project timeline pinned to his office wall, his purple goatee twitching as he looked at the list of mapped out tasks.

The project was progressing well, but wondered: Would the people of DataNova embrace this change?

"Technology is just half the battle," he murmured, reaching for his phone. "What we really need to do is to win over hearts and minds."

Uungu worked with Kijani, who was becoming an indispensable part of his project team.

"We need to tell a story," he began, "A story that makes every employee at DataNova see themselves as part of this CRM journey."

They spent the afternoon crafting a narrative that went beyond features and functions, focusing instead on how Salesforce would empower employees and transform customer relationships. Uungu insisted on tailoring the message for different departments.

Jade from Marketing suggested creating a series of short videos featuring employees discussing their hopes and expectations for the new CRM.

"Let's make this personal," she said.

Uungu nodded enthusiastically. "Brilliant. And let's not shy away from addressing concerns. We need to be transparent about the challenges as well as the benefits."

With the change narrative taking shape, Uungu began to think about the training plan. "We can't just dump a new system on people and expect them to figure it out," he said.

Amar proposed a multi-tiered approach. "Different roles will need different levels of expertise. We should tailor our training accordingly."

Uungu agreed, and they set about designing a training program that included:

- *Role-based training modules*
- *Hands-on workshops with real-world scenarios*
- *A library of short, task-specific video tutorials*
- *A "training sandbox" where employees could safely practice and experiment*

"And let's identify a few CRM champions," Uungu added. "They'll be our front-line support and change agents."

As they finalised the training plan, Uungu emphasised the importance of making it engaging. "This isn't just about transferring knowledge. It's about building confidence and excitement."

* * *

As the implementation progressed, Uungu realised they needed to generate excitement and demonstrate value even before the full launch.

"We need some quick wins," he told the team. "Something tangible that shows the potential of this new system."

They brainstormed ideas and decided to roll out a simplified version of the new customer dashboard to the sales team ahead of the full launch. The response was overwhelmingly positive, with sales reps raving about the improved visibility into customer interactions.

Energised by this success, Uungu turned his attention to planning the go-live celebration. "This isn't just a technical milestone," he insisted. "It's a transformational moment for DataNova. We need to mark it accordingly."

They planned a company-wide launch event, complete with interactive demos, recognition for key contributors, and even a "CRM quest" - a gamified challenge that encouraged employees to explore the new system.

As the build phase neared its end, Uungu looked at his team with pride. They hadn't just built a CRM system; they'd laid the groundwork for a cultural shift at DataNova.

"We have to remember that change doesn't happen in the system. It happens in the hearts and minds of our people. And we've given them every reason to embrace this change."

The stage was set for a transformation that went far beyond software – a transformation of how DataNova worked, collaborated, and served its customers.

Skills Development and User Engagement

The human element is often the determining factor in the success or failure of a CRM implementation. By focusing on effective change management, engaging training, and sustained user adoption, organisations can maximise the value of their CRM investment and drive long-term success.

Craft a Compelling Change Narrative

Effective communication is crucial for managing change and driving adoption. To create impactful communication strategies:

- Use storytelling to illustrate real-world benefits and successes
- Develop role-specific messaging that highlights relevant benefits for each user group
- Utilise a multi-channel approach (e.g., email, town halls (or company-wide meetings, videos, internal social media)
- Identify and leverage internal influencers to champion the CRM
- Be transparent about challenges and how they will be addressed

Failing to tailor communications can lead to disengagement and resistance to change. However, it is important to ensure transparency and integrity when communicating as they convey sincerity.

Adopt an Experiential Learning Approach

Hands-on, practical training is key to building user confidence and competence. To implement effective experiential learning:

- Create a safe 'sandbox' environment for users to practice without fear of mistakes

- Develop role-specific scenarios that mirror real-world tasks and challenges
- Implement gamification elements to make learning engaging and memorable such as Salesforce Trailhead[28]
- Offer a mix of learning formats (e.g., instructor-led, self-paced, peer-to-peer)
- Use actual company data in training to make it more relevant and impactful

Neglecting hands-on, practical training can result in users feeling overwhelmed and unprepared to use the CRM effectively.

Generate Momentum with Early Wins and Celebration

Building and maintaining enthusiasm throughout the implementation process is crucial for long-term adoption. To create momentum:

- Identify and implement quick wins that demonstrate immediate value
- Plan a comprehensive go-live celebration to mark the transformational moment. This can be done in internal organisation comms tool such as Slack or Teams
- Recognise and reward key contributors and early adopters
- Create engaging activities that encourage system exploration and utilisation
- Continuously communicate success stories and positive impacts across the organisation

Failing to celebrate milestones and early successes can lead to waning enthusiasm and slower adoption rates.

In my many years in the consulting industry, I've seen the power of celebration in driving CRM success. I recall a project with a mid-sized

---

[28] The Salesforce Trailhead is a great example of a gamified platform that helps people learn Salesforce skills and earn certifications through interactive, self-paced modules, trails and projects.

telecoms company where morale was low due to previous failed technology initiatives.

This was during the 2008 Olympic opening ceremony in Beijing. I can remember cake and balloons and Olympic themed launch activities which were very exciting and made it memorable for the end users (and myself!)

The lesson? Never underestimate the power of making CRM implementation fun and engaging. By turning it into a positive, shared experience, you can overcome scepticism and create a culture of enthusiasm around your CRM.

Remember, people are more likely to embrace change when they're enjoying the journey.

15
Go-Live Preparation and Execution

I think donuts and cakes are never optional at project go-live!

Uungu stood at the whiteboard, feeling a sense of anticipation as he wrote "Go-Live Countdown" at the top.

The Salesforce project had been a journey of challenges and triumphs, but now they were approaching the final hurdle: Go-Live.

Uungu turned to Vi, the Project Manager from Cloudacious. "I need to put together a Go-Live plan. Can you share with me your side of the production deployment plan for your team? I need to make sure our activity aligns with yours."

Over the next few days, they meticulously crafted a detailed Go-Live plan and checklist for DataNova. Uungu insisted on breaking down every task, no matter how small. "I want to know who's responsible for each item, when it needs to be done, and how we'll verify it's complete," he told the team.

Uungu paid particular attention to the cutover plan - the critical period when they'd switch from the old systems to the new CRM.

"We need to know exactly how long each step will take and everyone needs to know what to do in case we encounter a hiccup."

With the technical aspects taking shape, Uungu started to focus more on stakeholder communication.

He set up a series of meetings with key stakeholders across DataNova, from C-level executives to department heads and end-users.

In a meeting with Zamba, the CEO, Uungu was frank about what to expect. "There will be disruptions," he said. "We're transforming how our sales department operates. But we have plans in place to minimise and quickly address any issues."

Uungu worked with Jade from Marketing to activate a comprehensive communication plan:

- *Regular updates to all staff on Go-Live progress*
- *Clear instructions for what each department needs to do before and during Go-Live*
- *A dedicated channel for urgent communications*
- *Plans for announcing the successful launch of the new system*

As Go-Live day approached, Uungu's focus shifted to ensuring that the launch was ready. Working alongside Vi, they both made sure that all teams were prepared for their roles during the cutover.

The atmosphere was tense but exciting.

"Alright, everyone," Vi said, her voice steady. "We've prepared for this. We have our plan, our communications are in place, and we're ready to execute. "

At noon – the agreed time for go-live, the cutover process began.

Hours ticked by, each successful step bringing a small cheer from the team.

There were tense moments - a data migration hiccup that Coco quickly resolved causing a brief panic, but their meticulous planning paid off.

Finally, after many hours of feverish activity, Vi turned to Uungu with a broad smile. "We're live," she said simply.

Uungu let out a breath he felt like he'd been holding for weeks. He looked around at his tired but jubilant team, feeling an immense sense of pride.

"Great work, everyone," he said. "We've done it. Our new Salesforce CRM is now live."

As the team broke into applause and congratulations, Uungu allowed himself a moment of satisfaction. They had successfully navigated the Go-Live challenge. The new chapter in DataNova's digital transformation had begun.

CRM Launch Readiness and Deployment

The Go-Live phase is a critical juncture that can make or break a project. Here are a few things to consider:

The Comprehensive Go-Live Plan and Checklist

A detailed Go-Live plan is essential for managing the complexity of the launch process.

To create an effective Go-Live plan:

- Break down the launch process into detailed, actionable tasks
- Assign clear ownership and deadlines for each task
- Include all aspects of the launch: technical, operational, and organisational
- Develop a detailed cutover plan for the transition from old to new systems
- Create contingency plans for potential issues or delays
- Establish clear go/no-go criteria for the project at the end of UAT

Ensure all key stakeholders are fully aware of their responsibilities and deadlines.

I've seen a project where a critical resource, who had administrative access necessary for a crucial task for go-live, was unavailable on the scheduled day because vital emails landed in his spam folder, and the project manager failed to confirm receipt.

As a result, the person with the important admin access was on vacation during the project go-live!

You can see why it is essential for project managers to meticulously plan and oversee this critical phase to prevent such oversights.

A lack of detailed planning can easily lead to confusion and delays during the critical transition phase, particularly if the project manager hasn't thoroughly double-checked and confirmed that every step and resource is properly prepared.

Stakeholder Communication and Expectation Management

Clear communication is crucial for managing expectations and ensuring organisational readiness.

To effectively manage communication and expectations:

- Execute the 'implementing go-live' part of the communication plan to all relevant stakeholders
- Clearly articulate the benefits and potential challenges of the new CRM
- Provide regular updates on Go-Live progress and any changes to the plan
- Offer clear guidance on what different teams need to do before and during Go-Live
- Ensure leadership visibly supports the launch and change process
- Plan for how you'll announce and celebrate a successful launch

I recall a project where poor communication led to widespread anxiety and resistance among end-users.

Poor communication includes any communication that is inaccurate, untimely, incomplete or incorrect. Make sure that your communication plan is part of your change management strategy.

Readiness Checks and Final Preparations

Rigorous testing and preparation in the lead-up to Go-Live are critical for identifying and addressing potential issues.

In addition to User Acceptance Testing discussed in the previous chapter, here are a few things to consider to ensure readiness for launch (especially if within scope of signed-off requirements):

Project implementation

- Perform full system integration tests under realistic conditions
- Conduct load testing to ensure performance under peak usage
- Carry out security audits and penetration testing
- Verify that all teams understand their roles during the cutover process
- Ensure that support team is onboarded and in place

Projects that rush through final testing are likely to result in issues and bugs that can emerge immediately after launch, which can damage user confidence in the new system.

Go-Live is a significant organisational change.

Thorough preparation, clear communication, and robust support are essential for ensuring that your CRM launch marks the beginning of a successful digital transformation journey.

What happens after go-live? Make sure you have a robust plan for transitioning to post go-live support as part of your launch readiness checklist.

After Go-Live

After Go-Live

16
Hypercare and Stabilisation

Always plan for post go-live support and capability building early unless you love last-minute anxiety and stress!

Discovery · *Build* · *Test* · *Go Live!* · *Support*

@OnThePeiColl

Oh no! What comes after go-live?

Business as Usual (BAU) operations come after Go-Live.
Plan early and make provisions for the transition.

After Go-Live

The initial excitement of a successful CRM Go-Live for DataNova's Sales team had barely subsided when Uungu found himself facing a new challenge: ensuring the smooth operation and stabilisation of the new system.

As he settled into the command centre set up for the two-week Hypercare phase, he knew the coming days would be crucial.

"Team," Uungu addressed the assembled group of DataNova staff and Cloudacious experts, "Our system is live, but now we need to focus on stabilising the CRM for our Sales team and transitioning to steady-state support."

No sooner had Uungu finished speaking than the first email alert came in. A sales rep was having trouble accessing customer records. Uungu turned to Vi from Cloudacious. "Let's see how our issue resolution process holds up."

They quickly triaged the issue, determining it was a permissions problem affecting a small group of users.

Within minutes, they had a fix in place and were monitoring to ensure it solved the problem.

As more issues arose, Uungu insisted on a strict prioritisation process.

"We need to focus on business-critical issues first," he reminded the team. "Anything that impedes our sales team from doing their jobs takes top priority."

He set up a daily review meeting to go through all reported issues, ensuring nothing was overlooked and that they were addressing root causes, not just symptoms.

As the Hypercare phase advanced, Uungu shifted his focus to system performance and user adoption within the Sales team.

He worked closely with Amar and his IT team to set up comprehensive monitoring dashboards.

"I want to see real-time data on system response times, sales user logins, and key sales transaction volumes," Uungu explained.

When the dashboards revealed an unexpected spike in system load during mid-morning, Uungu investigated further. He discovered that the entire sales team was generating quotes simultaneously, causing a temporary slowdown.

On the user adoption front, Uungu was proactive in gathering feedback. He instituted daily check-ins with sales managers and randomly selected sales reps to gauge how they were adapting to the new system.

When he noticed that the adoption rate among senior sales executives was lagging, Uungu took immediate action.

He personally met with them, listening to their concerns and working with Cloudacious to adjust some workflows that were causing frustration.

As the two-week Hypercare phase came to an end, Uungu oversaw the transition to steady-state support managed by Cloudacious. However, he was already thinking ahead to the three-month review.

* * *

In the weeks that followed, Uungu became increasingly aware of the need to build DataNova's internal capability to support and optimise the CRM.

"We can't rely on Cloudacious indefinitely for all levels of support," he told Zamba during one of their update meetings. "We need to ensure our team can handle first-level support independently to reduce costs and improve response times."

Uungu worked with Clem and Vi from Cloudacious to develop a comprehensive knowledge transfer plan. They set up shadowing sessions where DataNova's IT staff could learn from Cloudacious experts as they resolved first-level support issues for the Sales team.

He also instituted a "teach, don't just fix" policy.

Whenever a Cloudacious team member solved a problem, they were required to document the process and walk a DataNova staff member through it.

To further build internal capability, Uungu organised a series of in-depth training sessions on various aspects of Salesforce and encouraged users to learn on Trailhead.

He made sure to include not just IT staff, but also select sales team members who showed aptitude and interest in becoming power users and potential first-level support resources.

As the three-month review approached, Uungu could see the progress they had made.

System issues were becoming less frequent and were increasingly resolved by DataNova's own staff.

User adoption among the Sales team was steadily climbing, and he was hearing more reports of how the new CRM was improving sales efficiency and customer relationship management.

In the review meeting with Cloudacious, Uungu presented his plan for DataNova to take over first-level support.

"We've built a solid foundation of internal knowledge," he said. "It's time we leveraged that to reduce our support costs and increase our self-sufficiency."

As the meeting concluded, Uungu felt a sense of accomplishment, mixed with anticipation for the road ahead.

The post-go-live phase had been intense, but it had established a solid foundation for DataNova's Salesforce journey. Now, it was time to start realising the full potential of their investment in the Sales team's new Salesforce system.

Post-Go-Live Support and Capability Building

The post-go-live phase, including Hypercare and the transition to steady-state support, is crucial for ensuring the long-term success of the system.

Hypercare Issue Resolution and Prioritisation Processes

Quick and efficient problem-solving is critical during the Hypercare phase to maintain user confidence and system stability, especially for critical business functions like Sales. This Hypercare phase is usually run by the partner before handing the system over to the client but the following still stands.

To ensure effective issue resolution:

- Implement a clear and accessible system for users to report issues
- Establish a triage process to quickly assess and prioritise reported problems
- Define clear escalation paths for different types of issues
- Set up a dedicated team with the authority to make quick decisions
- Conduct daily review meetings to ensure no issues fall through the cracks
- Focus on identifying and addressing root causes, not just symptoms

Monitoring of System Performance and User Adoption

Close monitoring during the post-go-live phase is essential for proactively identifying and addressing potential issues that could impact business operations.

To effectively monitor your CRM:

- Set up real-time dashboards for key performance metrics (e.g., response times, sales transaction volumes)
- Track user adoption rates and usage patterns across different sales roles
- Implement automated alerts for performance thresholds or unusual activity
- Regularly gather feedback from sales team members through surveys and check-ins
- Use monitoring insights to guide system optimisations and user training

I recall a project where we failed to monitor sales user adoption closely during the first few months after go-live.

We later discovered that a key group of sales executives had developed workarounds instead of using the new system, significantly reducing the CRM's effectiveness! Some even went back to using their old spreadsheets!

Knowledge Transfer and Building Internal Support Capability

Developing in-house expertise is crucial for long-term CRM success, reducing dependence on external support, and managing costs effectively.

To build internal capability:

- Develop a comprehensive knowledge transfer plan with your implementation partner
- Implement a "teach, don't just fix" approach when resolving issues
- Organise shadowing sessions where internal staff learn from external experts
- Conduct in-depth training sessions on various aspects of the CRM system
- Identify and nurture potential power users within the sales team to assist with first-level support

After Go-Live

- Create and maintain detailed documentation of processes and solutions

This is also an opportunity for the project team to have a post-mortem to learn from project mistakes and help make the transition to support a smoother one.

The post-go-live phase is not just about fixing problems – it's an opportunity to fine-tune your system, build internal capabilities, and drive user adoption within critical business functions like Sales.

Approach this phase with the same level of commitment and resources as the initial implementation.

Your investment in this critical period will pay dividends in the form of a stable, widely-adopted CRM system that delivers real value to your sales operations.

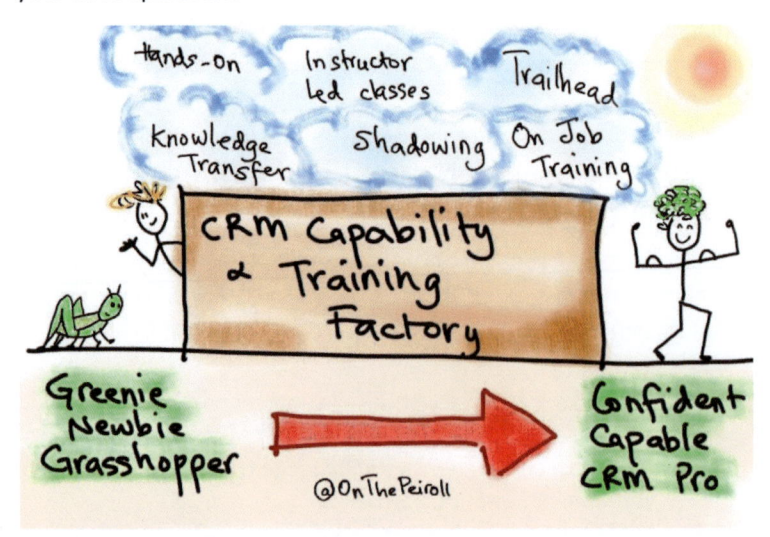

Building your internal capability is the first step in creating your own Centre of Excellence (CoE) - a dedicated team that governs and optimises the Salesforce implementation to provide long term business value.

17
Planning for Continuous Improvement

Kaizen is a continuous process of improvement using the - Plan, Do, Check, Act (Fix) process, and stabilising that improvement by making it the way things are done (standardising) to ensure change that sticks.

After Go-Live

Uungu studied the latest performance reports displayed on his monitor, taking note of the system's stability metrics and user adoption rates. The numbers were encouraging, but as he analysed the data more closely, he identified several opportunities for enhancement.

"We've established a strong foundation," he reflected, "but there's potential for more impact."

He scheduled a meeting with his core team in the project room. As Azul, Jade, and Amar settled into their seats, Uungu pulled up the latest system analytics on the screen.

"Our Salesforce implementation is performing well," he began, pointing to key metrics, "but I see opportunities to increase its value. Let's discuss how we can push it further."

Jade from Marketing leaned forward, her expression thoughtful. "My team has identified several potential report enhancements that could improve our pipeline visibility. But I'm not sure how we should prioritise these against other departments' needs."

"That's exactly what we need to address," Uungu replied.

"We need a structured process for handling enhancement requests. Without it, we risk either overlooking valuable improvements or implementing changes that don't align with our strategic priorities."

The team spent the next hour developing a comprehensive enhancement management process.

Amar suggested creating an online form for submission requests, while Azul emphasised the importance of clear business case documentation.

"Each request needs to demonstrate tangible value," Uungu agreed, sketching out their process on the whiteboard. We'll need initial screening by the IT team to assess technical feasibility, followed by review from a cross-functional committee."

"Monthly reviews might be too infrequent," Azul pointed out. "Some enhancements could be time-sensitive."

"Good point," Uungu acknowledged.

"Let's have monthly reviews for standard requests but include a fast-track option for urgent business-critical enhancements."

Their discussion shifted when Amar raised concerns about system maintenance. "While we're planning improvements, we need to ensure our foundation stays solid. I propose implementing regular health checks."

Uungu nodded, appreciating the CTO's foresight.

Together, they outlined a quarterly health check protocol that would examine everything from performance metrics to data quality. The protocol would include automated monitoring where possible, complemented by manual reviews of critical systems.

"We should also conduct regular security audits," Amar added. "Salesforce updates frequently, and we need to ensure our customisations maintain security best practices."

As they discussed resource allocation for these health checks, Uungu suggested rotating responsibilities among the IT team members.

"This approach serves two purposes," he explained. "It distributes the workload and helps build broader system knowledge across the team."

The conversation took an interesting turn when Azul brought up user proficiency. "Our sales team is using basic features effectively, but there's so much more Salesforce could do for us. We're barely scratching the surface of its capabilities."

This observation sparked an animated discussion about continuous learning. The team worked together to design a comprehensive training program that would cater to different learning styles and experience levels.

"Monthly power user workshops could help with advanced features," Jade suggested, "but we also need ongoing support for newer users."

"What about creating a library of short video tutorials?" Amar proposed. "Users could access them whenever they need a refresher on specific features."

Uungu expanded on these ideas, suggesting a mentorship program that would pair experienced users with newcomers. "And we could add

After Go-Live

some gamification elements," he added, "perhaps a points system for completing training modules or helping colleagues."

"We should also encourage formal Salesforce certifications," Uungu continued. "It gives the team concrete goals and validates their expertise."

Anticipating concerns about the time investment these initiatives would require, Uungu presented a clear connection to their business metrics.

"Every hour invested in training should show returns in improved sales cycles and operational efficiency. We'll track these metrics rigorously to demonstrate the ROI."

* * *

By the end of the meeting, they had developed a comprehensive plan that addressed both technical maintenance and user development. The plan balanced immediate needs with long-term strategic goals, ensuring their Salesforce system would continue to evolve with DataNova's growth.

Azul leaned back in her chair, tucking her blue hair behind her ear. She looked at Uungu with a mix of pride and amusement.

"You're twirling your goatee a little less these days Uung, " she said playfully. "You must be feeling some pride in what we've done here. You were instrumental in getting us to this point."

Uungu instinctively touched his whiskery chin, cracking a smile. "It's been quite a journey, hasn't it?"

"Indeed it has," Azul replied, remembering the challenges they'd overcome and the victories they'd celebrated.

As the team gathered their materials to leave, Uungu felt a deep sense of accomplishment tinged with anticipation for what lay ahead. They had transformed not just their systems but their entire approach to customer relationship management.

"By continuously refining and expanding our use of Salesforce," he reflected, "we're not just maintaining our investment – we're multiplying its value for DataNova's future."

Key Practices for Ongoing Success

Continuous improvement is crucial for ensuring long-term success and maximising ROI because the journey doesn't end with go-live.

The Feedback and Enhancement Process

A formal process for collecting and acting on user feedback is crucial for continuous improvement. To implement an effective feedback and enhancement process:

- Create an easily accessible system for users to submit enhancement requests
- Establish a cross-functional committee to review requests, make risk and impact assessments and prioritise requests
- Develop clear criteria for evaluating enhancement requests, including potential ROI and strategic alignment[29]
- Implement regular cycles for reviewing and implementing approved enhancements
- Communicate status of enhancement requests transparently
- Celebrate and showcase implemented improvements to encourage ongoing engagement

If you don't have a structured process for handling user feedback, it could lead to a backlog of unaddressed requests and growing user frustration. As such, it's always a good idea to have a well-defined enhancement process that keeps users engaged and the system evolving.

---

[29] Many organisations set up Change Advisory Boards (CABs), a committee made up of business and technology leaders from different departments of the organisation and serves to guide and oversee change management initiatives. Organisations that have complex enterprise IT environments benefit from having enterprise architects who are important in can help ensure alignment with business strategy, adherence to governance, compliance and well-architected frameworks which aims to deliver true business value and mitigate risks in the long run.

Regular System Health Checks

Proactive monitoring and maintenance are essential for ensuring ongoing CRM performance and reliability. Here are some ways to implement effective system health checks:

- Develop a comprehensive checklist covering performance, data quality, usage patterns, security, and integrations
- Schedule regular (e.g., quarterly) health check reviews
- Automate data collection for health checks where possible
- Include both technical metrics and user satisfaction measures
- Establish clear ownership and accountability for addressing identified issues
- Use health check insights to inform your enhancement and optimisation efforts

Ongoing Training and Skill Development

Continuous learning is key to maximising the value of your CRM investment.

To create an effective ongoing training program:

- Offer a variety of learning formats to cater for different learning styles (e.g., workshops, video tutorials, mentoring)
- Develop role-specific training paths
- Implement a certification programme to recognise and incentivise Salesforce expertise
- Regularly update training content to cover new features and best practices
- Tie training efforts to specific KPIs to demonstrate ROI

Continuous improvement is not just about technology – it's about people, processes, and a commitment to ongoing excellence. Approach it as a core part of your CRM strategy, not an afterthought.

A final word from Pei

A final word from Pei

I love it that you've got this far.

Thank you for joining Uungu on his journey through the lifecycle of implementing a Salesforce project for DataNova.

Whether you're a project sponsor, a business stakeholder, or someone tasked with shepherding a CRM implementation - I hope this book has given you practical insights and confidence to tackle the challenges ahead.

Throughout my career, I've learned that successful projects aren't just about technology or methodology - they're fundamentally about people.

The most sophisticated CRM system in the world won't deliver value if people don't use it, and the most detailed project plan won't succeed without strong relationships and trust.

Every time I start a new project, I remind myself that behind every requirement, every user story, and every change request is a human being trying to do their job better.

Understanding their hopes, fears, and motivations is just as important as understanding their business processes.

Life in project delivery can be chaotic and unpredictable. There will be unexpected challenges, difficult conversations, and moments of doubt.

So I'll leave you with a few final tips:

- Take time to build relationships.
- Create safe spaces for honest dialogue.
- Celebrate small wins along the way.

And most importantly - take care of yourself and your team throughout the journey.

Thank you for reading my book.

Remember - behind every successful project is a team of people who cared enough to make it happen.

Be one of those people.
x Pei

Appendix

Appendix

Sample Business Case

The Business Case for DataNova's Salesforce Implementation

Prepared by Uungu, Project Manager

1. Executive Summary

DataNova, our market intelligence company, has experienced remarkable growth over the past few years. However, this success has exposed limitations in our current systems and processes, particularly in managing client relationships and sales operations. This business case proposes implementing Salesforce, a leading Customer Relationship Management (CRM) system, to address these challenges and position DataNova for continued growth.

After thorough analysis, I strongly recommend engaging an external Salesforce partner for this implementation. While this approach involves a higher initial investment, it offers several critical advantages:

1. Faster time-to-value, allowing us to realise benefits sooner
2. Reduced implementation risk due to specialised expertise
3. Access to best practices and industry-specific solutions
4. Minimal disruption to our current operations

The proposed CRM implementation is expected to yield a 93% ROI in the first year, with ongoing benefits in efficiency, sales performance, and client satisfaction.

2. Business Need

Problem Statement

DataNova's rapid growth has exposed critical weaknesses in our current systems:

1. Inefficient Client Information Management: Valuable client data is scattered across individual email accounts, Google Sheets, and shared drives, leading to information silos and lost opportunities.
2. Duplicate Outreach: We've had three incidents in the past month where different account executives contacted the same potential client, damaging our professional image.
3. Time-Consuming Reporting: As Kijani pointed out, "Pulling together a sales report for Azul every week is such a pain. I have to get everyone to update their stuff on their Google Sheets, and then I have to collate the info, and it just takes aaaages!"
4. Lack of Process Standardisation: With our growth, we can no longer rely on informal, ad-hoc processes for managing client relationships and sales pipelines.
5. Limited Visibility: Management lacks real-time insights into sales performance and pipeline health, hindering strategic decision-making.

Strategic Alignment

Implementing a CRM system directly supports several of DataNova's strategic objectives:

1. Scaling Operations: As Azul noted, "We can't go back. It was ok to be scrappy in the beginning, but now that we've grown so much – our systems need to be able to scale as well."
2. Maintaining Service Quality: By centralising client information, we can provide more personalised and responsive service, even as we grow.
3. Improving Sales Efficiency: Streamlined processes will allow our sales team to focus more on building relationships and less on administrative tasks.
4. Enhancing Decision-Making: Better data and analytics will support more informed strategic decisions.

Current Situation Analysis

Our current setup includes:

- Google Sheets for tracking client interactions and sales pipelines
- Shared Google Drive folders for storing reports and client information
- Email as the primary tool for client communication and internal collaboration
- This system worked when we were a small team of five, but with our current staff of 50+ and hundreds of clients, it's leading to:
- Lost productivity: Estimated 5 hours per week per sales rep spent on administrative tasks
- Missed opportunities: At least two major deals in Q2 were lost due to poor follow-up
- Data inconsistencies: 30% of client records have outdated or conflicting information
- Reporting delays: Weekly sales reports take an average of 6 hours to compile

3. Scope and Objectives

Project Scope

The CRM implementation will encompass:

1. Sales Process Management

- Lead and opportunity tracking
- Sales pipeline visualisation
- Automated task creation and assignment

2. Client Interaction Tracking

- Centralised client information database
- Communication history (emails, calls, meetings)
- Document management for client-related files

3. Reporting and Analytics

- Real-time dashboards for sales performance
- Custom report generation

- Predictive analytics for sales forecasting

4. System Integration
    - Email integration (Gmail)
    - Calendar sync
    - Integration with our market research database

5. Mobile Access
    - Full-featured mobile app for on-the-go access

Objectives

1. Efficiency: Increase sales team productivity by 20% within six months of implementation
    - Measure: Time spent on administrative tasks vs. client interaction

2. Data Quality: Achieve 98% data accuracy in client records within three months
    - Measure: Regular data audits and user feedback

3. Outreach Coordination: Reduce duplicate outreach incidents to zero within the first month
    - Measure: Reported incidents of uncoordinated client contact

4. Reporting Efficiency: Decrease time spent on weekly sales reporting by 80%
    - Measure: Time taken to generate and distribute weekly sales reports

5. Sales Performance: Improve lead conversion rate by 15% within the first year
    - Measure: Conversion rate of qualified leads to closed deals

6. User Adoption: Achieve 90% user adoption rate within three months of go-live
    - Measure: Regular system usage metrics and user surveys

Appendix

4. Options Analysis

Option 1: In-House Implementation
Resources Required:

- 2 full-time developers with Salesforce expertise (to be hired)
- 1 full-time project manager (Uungu)
- Part-time involvement from 3 sales team members for requirements and testing
- Part-time support from 1 IT staff member

Capabilities Assessment:

- Our current IT team has no specific Salesforce experience
- We would need to hire or train Salesforce developers
- Project management can be handled internally, but there's a steep learning curve for Salesforce-specific best practices

Timeline:

- Month 1-2: Team hiring and onboarding
- Month 3-4: Requirements gathering and system design
- Month 5-7: Development and configuration
- Month 8-9: Testing and refinement
- Month 10: User training and go-live

Total estimated timeline: 10 months

Cost Estimation:

- New hires (2 Salesforce professionals, 1 x admin, 1 x developer): $220,000/year
- Additional training for internal team: $20,000
- Salesforce licenses: $50,000/year[30]
- Misc. tools and expenses: $10,000

Total first-year cost: $300,000

---

[30] Obviously you can tell I've made this up!

Option 2: External Salesforce Partner

Vendor Capabilities:

We've spoken to a few Salesforce implementation partners and discussed our high-level requirements to get a ballpark figure of what the project implementation would look like. All have extensive experience, but Cloudacious and CloudMasters both stand out due to their:

- 10+ years of Salesforce implementation experience
- Specific expertise in the market research industry
- Strong customer references and case studies
- Comprehensive training and change management approach

Implementation Approach:

Both have very similar approach to the project delivery:

1. Discovery (3 weeks): Requirements gathering, current process analysis

2. Implementation (12 weeks): Configuration, customisation, data migration, integration

3. Deployment (5 weeks): User acceptance testing, training, go-live support

Cost Estimation:

- Discovery $40,000 (for two partners)
- Implementation services: $180,000*
- Salesforce licenses: $50,000/year
- Ongoing support (first year): $30,000

Total first-year cost: $300,000

* Note that this cost will be validated after the discovery process has been concluded

Timeline: Approximately 5 months from project kick-off to go-live

Risk Assessment:

- Dependency on vendor mitigated by clear contract terms and regular milestones

Appendix

- Knowledge transfer plan included to build internal capabilities
- Faster implementation reduces risk of project fatigue and scope creep

5. Cost-Benefit Analysis

Costs

Category	In-House	External Partner
Implementation	$250,000	$220,000
Licenses	$50,000	$50,000
Ongoing Support	N/A (internal)	$30,000
Total First Year	$300,000	$300,000

Benefits

1. Time Savings:

   - 5 hours/week saved per sales rep (20 reps) = 5,200 hours/year[31]
   - At $50/hour average rate = $260,000 annual productivity gain

2. Increased Sales:

   - 15% improvement in lead conversion
   - Based on last year's new business ($5M), additional $750,000 in annual revenue
   - At 40% profit margin = $300,000 additional profit

3. Avoided Costs:

   - Eliminate need for multiple tool subscriptions: $20,000/year savings

---

[31] Am assuming 260 working days in a year in this fictional world where everyone works super hard and never gets sick! (In reality, there are 220 working days a year in the UK – not sure about other countries).

Appendix

4. Intangible Benefits:

- Improved client satisfaction and loyalty
- Better team morale and reduced frustration
- Enhanced company image and professionalism

Total Annual Benefits: $580,000

ROI Calculation per year

Category	In-House	External Partner
Total Benefits	$580,000	$580,000
Total Costs	$300,000	$300,000
Net Benefit	$280,000	$280,000
ROI	93%	93%

While the ROI is identical for both options in the first year, the external partner option allows us to realise these benefits 5 months sooner and with less risk.[32]

6. Risk Assessment

Category	In-House	External Partner	Mitigation Strategy
Implementation Failure	High	Low	• Choose experienced partner with proven track record • Clear project governance and regular check-ins
Timeline Overrun	High	Medium	• Detailed project plan with buffers • Regular progress reviews • Change control process
Budget Overrun	Medium	Medium	• Fixed-price contract with clearly defined scope • Change request process for out-of-scope items

---

[32] The cost savings of having the system 5 months earlier could also be quantified in the business case to make it stronger but I decided not to.

Appendix

Category	In-House	External Partner	Mitigation Strategy
Poor User Adoption	Medium	Low	• Comprehensive change management plan • Phased rollout approach • Ongoing training and support
Data Migration Issues	High	Medium	• Thorough data cleansing before migration • Pilot migration with subset of data • Validation and reconciliation process
Loss of Internal Control	Low	Medium	• Clear governance structure • Knowledge transfer plan • Documentation of all customisations

7. Resource Requirements[33]

In-House Resources

- 1 Project Manager (Uungu) 100% time allocation
- 2 Salesforce Developers 100% time allocation (to be hired)
- 1 Business Analyst 50% time allocation
- 3 Sales Team Subject Matter Experts 20% time allocation each
- 1 IT Support Staff 25% time allocation

External Resources (if using partner)

- 1 Project Manager (Uungu) 50% time allocation as internal point of contact
- 3 Sales Team Subject Matter Experts 10% time allocation each
- 1 IT Support Staff 15% time allocation

Training Needs

---

[33] In theory the costs for the resources should also be factored in for both options – e.g. The salary for Uungu and all resources pro-rated for the duration of the project should be added to the costs in the ROI calculation. However, this would require me to make up more numbers to justify a fictional business case and so I am just going to take a creative license on the math here.

- Salesforce Administrator training for 2 internal staff
- End-user training for all sales and customer service staff (approx. 30 people)
- Advanced reporting training for 5 managers

8. Implementation Timeline

External Partner Timeline

Phase	Duration	Key Activities
Discovery	2 weeks	• Kick-off meeting • Requirements workshops • Current state analysis • Future state definition
Design	3 weeks	• System architecture design • Data model definition • User interface design • Integration design
Implementation	10 weeks	• System configuration • Custom development • Data migration • Integration development • Unit testing
Deployment	5 weeks	• User acceptance testing • Training development and delivery • Go-live preparation • Cutover planning
Post Go-Live	4 weeks	• Hypercare support • Issue resolution • Performance tuning

Total duration: 24 weeks (approx. 5.5 months)

Appendix

9. Stakeholder Analysis

Stakeholder	Expectations	Concerns	Engagement Strategy
Azul (Sales Director)	• Improved sales efficiency • Better pipeline visibility	• Disruption to sales activities • ROI justification	• Regular project updates • Involvement in key decisions • Early access to new reports
Kijani (Sales Team Lead)	• Easier reporting • Better team coordination	• Learning curve for new system • Data migration accuracy	• Involvement in requirements gathering • Champion for user adoption • Feedback on UI design
IT Team	• Seamless integration • Data security	• System complexity • Ongoing maintenance	• Inclusion in technical discussions • Training on Salesforce administration • Clear support model definition
Leadership Team	• ROI achievement • Strategic alignment	• Project cost • Implementation risk	• Monthly steering committee meetings • Clear KPI tracking • Phased benefit realisation plan
Sales Team	• Simplified processes • Mobile access	• Increased data entry • Privacy of client relationships	• Regular communication on benefits • Hands-on training sessions • Feedback mechanisms

10. Recommendation

Based on the comprehensive analysis presented in this business case, I strongly recommend we proceed with the external Salesforce partner option by going to tender for a CRM discovery with two partners and reviewing the final outcome and proposal for the full project implementation before we commit to selecting our implementation partner.

Key factors supporting this recommendation:

1. Faster Time-to-Value: The external partner approach indicates that the solution can be implemented in about 5 months, compared to 10 months for the in-house option. This allows us to start realising benefits and ROI much sooner.
2. Risk Mitigation: Partners will have extensive experience with Salesforce implementations, particularly in our industry, which significantly reduces the risk of project failure or delays.
3. Expertise Access: We gain immediate access to a team of Salesforce experts, without the need to hire or extensively train our own staff.
4. Best Practices: External Salesforce partners will bring industry best practices and pre-built solutions that can accelerate our implementation and improve our processes.
5. Change Management: The partner's comprehensive training and change management approach will support better user adoption and minimise disruption to our operations.
6. Cost-Effective: While the first-year costs are similar, the partner option provides more value through faster implementation, reduced risk, and included support.
7. Scalability: The partner's solution will be designed with our growth in mind, ensuring the system can scale as DataNova continues to expand.

11. Next Steps

1. Present this business case to the leadership team for approval (Week 1)
2. If approved, launch the RFP for our CRM discovery
3. Select two Salesforce partners to run discoveries in parallel.
4. Finalise contract negotiations with discovery partners (Week 2-3)

5. Establish internal project team and allocate necessary resources (Week 4)
6. Conduct internal kick-off meeting to align all stakeholders (Week 5)
7. Begin discovery phase (Week 6)

12. Appendices

1. Detailed ROI calculations and assumptions
2. Vendor comparison matrix
3. Current system pain points survey results from sales team
4. Sample Salesforce dashboards and reports relevant to our business
5. Proposed project governance structure
6. Detailed project timeline and milestones
7. Change management and communication plan outline

Sample RFP

Request for Proposal (RFP)

CRM Implementation Discovery Phase for DataNova

1. Introduction

DataNova, a leading market intelligence company, is seeking proposals from qualified Salesforce implementation partners to conduct a comprehensive Discovery phase for our CRM implementation project. This Discovery will be crucial in designing a CRM system that enhances our client relationships, streamlines our sales processes, and supports our continued growth.

2. Company Background

DataNova delivers market research reports and customised intelligence solutions to a global client base. With a team of over 50 employees and hundreds of clients worldwide, we've outgrown our current systems and require a robust CRM solution to maintain our high standards of client service and operational efficiency.

3. Project Objectives

The primary objectives of this Discovery phase are to:

- Gain a deep understanding of DataNova's business processes and requirements
- Develop a comprehensive plan for CRM implementation
- Ensure alignment between DataNova's needs and the proposed Salesforce solution
- Provide DataNova with detailed documentation to support informed decision-making

4. Scope of Work

The selected partner will be responsible for conducting a thorough Discovery phase, including but not limited to:

Appendix

4.1 Requirements Gathering

- Conduct workshops and interviews with key stakeholders
- Document functional and non-functional requirements
- Identify pain points in current processes and systems

4.2 Analysis and Design

- Analyze current systems and data structures
- Develop high-level solution design
- Identify potential risks and mitigation strategies

4.3 Documentation and Deliverables

Produce comprehensive documentation including:

- Process flows
- System landscape
- Data model
- Security model
- Environment release strategy
- Data migration strategy
- User stories
- Test strategy
- Training plan
- Project plan
- Solution design document

4.4 Presentation

- Present findings and proposed solution to DataNova stakeholders
- 4.5 Transition Plan
- Provide a detailed approach for transitioning from Discovery to Implementation
- Include cost estimates for the full implementation phase

5. Detailed CRM Requirements

The proposed CRM solution should address the following requirements:

5.1 Contact Management:

- Ability to store and manage detailed client information

- Support for multiple contacts per account
- Custom fields for industry-specific data

5.2 Interaction Tracking:

- Log all client interactions (calls, emails, meetings)
- Integration with email clients for automatic logging
- Mobile app for on-the-go interaction logging

5.3 Sales Process Management:

- Customizable sales pipeline stages
- Automated task creation and assignment
- Deal tracking and forecasting

5.4 Reporting and Analytics:

- Customizable dashboards for different user roles
- Advanced reporting capabilities with visualisations
- Export functionality for further analysis

5.5 Team Collaboration:

- Internal messaging system
- Ability to share and collaborate on documents
- Task assignment and tracking

5.6 Email Integration:

- Two-way sync with popular email clients (e.g., Outlook, Gmail)
- Email templates for common communications
- Email tracking (opens, clicks)

5.7 Calendar Integration:

- Sync with popular calendar applications
- Meeting scheduling functionality

5.8 Document Management:

- Central repository for sales collateral and client documents
- Version control for documents
- Easy sharing of documents with clients

Appendix

5.9 Mobile Access:

- Full-featured mobile app for iOS and Android
- Offline access to key information

5.10 Data Import/Export:

- Bulk import/export capabilities

5.11 Customisation:

- Ability to customise fields, layouts, and workflows
- Support for custom modules or apps

5.12 Security:

- Role-based access control
- Data encryption at rest and in transit
- Two-factor authentication

5.13 Lead Management:

- Lead scoring capabilities
- Automated lead assignment
- Lead nurturing workflows

5.14 Account Planning:

- Tools for strategic account planning
- Relationship mapping for complex organisations

5.15 Territory Management:

- Ability to define and manage sales territories
- Automatic lead/account assignment based on territories

5.16 Forecasting:

- Sales forecasting tools
- Pipeline analysis

5.17 Training and Support:

- Comprehensive training materials
- Ongoing customer support (specify preferred support channels)

5.18 Data Migration:

- Assisted data migration from existing systems
- Data cleaning and deduplication services

5.19 Compliance:

- GDPR compliance features
- Audit trails for data changes

5.20 Localisation:

- Multi-language support
- Multi-currency support

5.21 Future Considerations (for phased approach):

- Integration with CPQ (Configure, Price, Quote) systems
- AI-powered insights and recommendations
- Predictive analytics for sales forecasting
- Social media profile enrichment for contacts
- Social listening capabilities

6. Proposal Requirements

Your proposal should include:

6.1 Company Information

- Brief history and background of your company
- Relevant experience in Salesforce implementations, particularly in the market research industry
- Client references

6.2 Discovery Approach

- Detailed methodology for conducting the Discovery phase
- Timeline for completing the Discovery and delivering all required documentation
- Team composition, including roles and expertise

6.3 Sample Deliverables

Examples of deliverables from previous Discovery phases (anonymised if necessary)

Appendix

6.4 Pricing

- Detailed breakdown of costs for the Discovery phase
- Any assumptions or caveats related to pricing

6.5 Transition to Implementation

- Proposed approach for transitioning from Discovery to Implementation
- Preliminary cost estimates for the full implementation phase

7. Evaluation Criteria

Proposals will be evaluated based on the following criteria:

- Methodology and approach to Discovery (30%)
- Quality of sample deliverables (20%)
- Team expertise and relevant experience (20%)
- Transition plan and implementation cost estimates (15%)
- Timeline and project management approach (10%)
- Discovery phase cost and value for money (5%)

8. Submission Instructions

Please submit your proposal electronically to rfp@datanova.com by [Insert Date].

9. Questions and Clarifications

A vendor conference call will be held on [Insert Date] at [Insert Time]. Please submit any questions in advance to questions@datanova.com by [Insert Date].

10. Selection Process

After reviewing the proposals, DataNova will shortlist partners to conduct the Discovery phase. Once all shortlisted partners have completed their Discoveries and presented their findings, proposed solutions, and implementation plans (including costs), DataNova will make a final decision on the implementation partner.

We look forward to your proposals and to selecting a partner who can help DataNova transform our client relationships and sales processes through a comprehensive and insightful Discovery phase, followed by a successful implementation.

Appendix

Sample Vendor Scoring Matrix

Criteria	Weight	Scoring Notes
Adherence to RFP Instructions		
Completeness of response	3	Score 1-5: 1 = Major sections missing, 5 = All sections complete and well-organised
Compliance with format requirements	2	Score 1-5: 1 = Incorrect format, 5 = Perfectly follows required format
Timeliness of submission	2	Score 1-5: 1 = Late submission, 5 = Submitted well before deadline
Quality of presentation	3	Score 1-5: 1 = Poor presentation, 5 = Professional and easy to navigate
Company Information		
Financial stability	3	Score 1-5: 1 = Concerning financials, 5 = Strong financial position
Years in business	2	Score 1-5: 1 = <2 years, 3 = 2-5 years, 5 = >5 years
Company size and resources	2	Score 1-5: 1 = Limited resources, 5 = Ample resources for project
Corporate culture and values alignment	3	Score 1-5: 1 = Misaligned values, 5 = Strong cultural fit
Software Demo		
User interface and experience	3	Score 1-5: 1 = Confusing UI, 5 = Intuitive and user-friendly
Functionality coverage	4	Score 1-5: 1 = Missing key functions, 5 = Exceeds functional requirements
Performance and speed	3	Score 1-5: 1 = Slow and unresponsive, 5 = Fast and efficient
Customisation showcased	3	Score 1-5: 1 = Limited customisation, 5 = Extensive, relevant customisation
Experience with Salesforce implementations		
Years of experience	3	Score 1-5: 1 = <2 years, 3 = 2-5 years, 5 = >5 years
Number of similar projects completed	3	Score 1-5: 1 = <5 projects, 3 = 5-15 projects, 5 = >15 projects
Industry-specific experience	3	Score 1-5: 1 = No industry experience, 5 = Extensive industry experience
Certifications and partnerships	3	Score 1-5: 1 = Basic certifications, 5 = Advanced certifications and strong partnership
Understanding of business requirements		

Appendix

Criteria	Weight	Scoring Notes
Clarity of requirement interpretation	3	Score 1-5: 1 = Misinterpreted requirements, 5 = Thorough understanding demonstrated
Alignment with business goals	3	Score 1-5: 1 = Misaligned solution, 5 = Solution perfectly aligned with goals
Identified potential challenges	3	Score 1-5: 1 = No challenges identified, 5 = Comprehensive risk assessment
Proposed solutions to challenges	3	Score 1-5: 1 = No solutions offered, 5 = Innovative and effective solutions proposed
Proposed implementation methodology		
Approach suitability	2	Score 1-5: 1 = Generic approach, 5 = Tailored to our specific needs
Clarity and detail of methodology	2	Score 1-5: 1 = Vague description, 5 = Clear, detailed methodology
Risk management strategy	2	Score 1-5: 1 = No risk management, 5 = Comprehensive risk mitigation plan
Quality assurance process	2	Score 1-5: 1 = Minimal QA, 5 = Robust QA throughout project
Project timeline and milestones		
Realistic timeline	3	Score 1-5: 1 = Unrealistic timeline, 5 = Well-planned, achievable timeline
Clear milestone definition	2	Score 1-5: 1 = Vague milestones, 5 = Specific, measurable milestones
Resource allocation plan	2	Score 1-5: 1 = Unclear resource plan, 5 = Detailed resource allocation
Flexibility for adjustments	2	Score 1-5: 1 = Rigid plan, 5 = Adaptable approach with clear change management
Team composition and expertise		
Team size and structure	2	Score 1-5: 1 = Inadequate team, 5 = Well-structured team with right size
Key personnel qualifications	3	Score 1-5: 1 = Underqualified team, 5 = Highly qualified key personnel
Relevant technical skills	3	Score 1-5: 1 = Limited technical skills, 5 = Comprehensive technical expertise
Project management expertise	2	Score 1-5: 1 = Inexperienced PM, 5 = Certified, experienced PM
Training and knowledge transfer plan		
Comprehensiveness of training	2	Score 1-5: 1 = Basic training offered, 5 = Comprehensive, role-based training
Variety of training methods	2	Score 1-5: 1 = Single training method, 5 = Multiple methods (e.g., hands-on, documentation, video)
Post-implementation support	2	Score 1-5: 1 = Limited support, 5 = Extensive ongoing support and training

Appendix

Criteria	Weight	Scoring Notes
Documentation quality	2	Score 1-5: 1 = Minimal documentation, 5 = Thorough, user-friendly documentation
Post-implementation support and maintenance		
Support availability (hours/response time)	2	Score 1-5: 1 = Limited availability, 5 = 24/7 support with quick response time
Maintenance schedule	2	Score 1-5: 1 = Reactive maintenance, 5 = Proactive maintenance schedule
Upgrade process	2	Score 1-5: 1 = Disruptive upgrades, 5 = Smooth, well-planned upgrade process
Issue resolution process	2	Score 1-5: 1 = Unclear process, 5 = Clear escalation and resolution procedures
Integration capabilities		
Experience with similar integrations	2	Score 1-5: 1 = No similar experience, 5 = Extensive experience with similar integrations
Proposed integration methods	2	Score 1-5: 1 = Basic integration, 5 = Advanced, efficient integration methods
Data synchronisation approach	2	Score 1-5: 1 = Manual sync, 5 = Automated, real-time synchronisation
Data migration approach		Score 1-5: 1 = No clear strategy, 5 = Clear, well-planned approach
API and middleware expertise		
Data cleaning strategy	2	Score 1-5: 1 = No cleaning strategy, 5 = Comprehensive data cleansing plan
Migration tools and techniques	2	Score 1-5: 1 = Basic tools, 5 = Advanced migration tools and techniques
Data validation process	2	Score 1-5: 1 = Minimal validation, 5 = Thorough validation process
Customisation and configuration abilities		Score 1-5: 1 = Limited experience, 5 = Comprehensive demonstration of capabilities
Handling of legacy data		
Understanding of required customisations	1	Score 1-5: 1 = Misunderstood requirements, 5 = Clear grasp of customisation needs
Approach to custom development	1	Score 1-5: 1 = Over-reliance on custom code, 5 = Balanced approach using platform features
Use of Salesforce platform features	2	Score 1-5: 1 = Minimal use of platform, 5 = Maximises platform capabilities
Scalability of customisations	1	Score 1-5: 1 = Non-scalable solutions, 5 = Highly scalable customisations

Appendix

Criteria	Weight	Scoring Notes
User adoption strategy		
Change management approach	1	Score 1-5: 1 = No change management, 5 = Comprehensive change management plan
User engagement plan	1	Score 1-5: 1 = Minimal user involvement, 5 = High user engagement throughout
Adoption measurement methods	2	Score 1-5: 1 = No measurement plan, 5 = Clear KPIs and measurement strategy
Ongoing user support	1	Score 1-5: 1 = Limited ongoing support, 5 = Continuous support and improvement
Pricing and cost structure		
Overall cost competitiveness	3	Score 1-5: 1 = Significantly overpriced, 5 = Highly competitive pricing
Pricing model clarity	2	Score 1-5: 1 = Confusing pricing, 5 = Clear, transparent pricing model
Payment terms	2	Score 1-5: 1 = Unfavourable terms, 5 = Flexible, favourable payment terms
Additional costs and fees	3	Score 1-5: 1 = Many hidden costs, 5 = All costs clearly outlined
References and case studies		
Relevance of references	1	Score 1-5: 1 = Irrelevant references, 5 = Highly relevant, recent references
Client satisfaction levels	2	Score 1-5: 1 = Low satisfaction reported, 5 = High client satisfaction across references
Demonstrated ROI in case studies	1	Score 1-5: 1 = No ROI data, 5 = Clear, impressive ROI demonstrated
Lessons learned from past projects	1	Score 1-5: 1 = No lessons shared, 5 = Valuable insights from past projects
Innovation and value-added services		
Innovative solutions proposed	1	Score 1-5: 1 = No innovation shown, 5 = Highly innovative, unique solutions
Additional services offered	1	Score 1-5: 1 = No additional services, 5 = Valuable complementary services
Continuous improvement approach	2	Score 1-5: 1 = No improvement plan, 5 = Clear strategy for ongoing enhancement
Future-proofing strategies	1	Score 1-5: 1 = No future planning, 5 = Strong vision for future developments
Total Score (140)	0	

Glossary

Term	Definition
Acceptance Criteria	Specific conditions that must be met for a feature or requirement to be considered complete and acceptable
Agile	A project management methodology that breaks work into short iterations with frequent feedback and adaptation
AppExchange	Salesforce's marketplace for pre-built applications and components
Business Analyst (BA)	Professional who analyses business needs and translates them into requirements and specifications
Business Case	Document justifying a project's investment by outlining costs, benefits, risks, and expected returns
Change Management	Structured approach to transitioning individuals and organizations to desired future states
CRM	Customer Relationship Management - system for managing relationships and interactions with customers
Custom Object	A database table created to store information specific to an organization's needs in Salesforce
Data Migration	Process of moving data from legacy systems to the new Salesforce system
Data Model	Structure defining how data is organized and related within the system
Defect	An error or flaw in the system where functionality doesn't work as specified in requirements
Discovery Phase	Initial project phase focused on understanding business needs and requirements
Enhancement Request	New feature or modification request that wasn't part of original requirements
Go-Live	The point at which a new system becomes operational and available to users
Governance Framework	Structure defining how decisions are made and who has authority to make them
Hypercare	Intensive support period immediately following system go-live
Implementation Partner	External company specializing in Salesforce implementations

Appendix

Term	Definition
Integration	Connection between Salesforce and other systems to share data
Iteration	Fixed time period (usually 2 weeks) for completing a set of development tasks
KPI	Key Performance Indicator - metric used to measure success
Legacy System	Existing older system being replaced or integrated with
MoSCoW	Prioritisation method (Must have, Should have, Could have, Won't have)
Out-of-the-Box	Standard Salesforce functionality available without customization
Power User	Advanced system user who can assist others and champion adoption
Project Charter	Document formally authorizing the project and outlining high-level parameters
Project Sponsor	Senior executive responsible for project success and removing obstacles
RAIDD Log	Risks, Assumptions, Issues, Dependencies, and Decisions tracking document
Release Strategy	Plan for how system functionality will be deployed to users
Requirements	Detailed specifications of what the system needs to do
REST API	Standard protocol for system integrations
Retrospective	Meeting to review what worked well and what could be improved
RFP	Request for Proposal - formal document requesting vendor proposals
ROI	Return on Investment - measure of project's financial benefits versus costs
Sandbox	Test environment for safely making and testing changes
Scope	Defined boundaries of what will and won't be included in the project
Scope Creep	Uncontrolled expansion of project scope beyond original parameters
Security Model	Framework defining who can access what data and functionality
Service Level Agreement (SLA)	Agreed standards for system support and issue resolution
Show and Tell	Regular demonstration of completed work to stakeholders
Solution Architect	Technical expert who designs the overall system solution
Stakeholder	Person or group with interest in or influence over the project

Appendix

Term	Definition
Stand-up	Brief daily meeting to discuss progress and obstacles
Statement of Work (SOW)	Document detailing work to be performed by vendor
Steering Committee	Group of senior stakeholders providing project oversight
System Integration	Connecting different systems to work together
Technical Debt	Future rework caused by choosing quick solutions over better approaches
Test Script	Step-by-step instructions for testing specific functionality
UAT	User Acceptance Testing - validation of system by end users
User Story	Description of functionality from end user perspective
Vendor	Company providing products or services for the project
War Room	Dedicated space for project team during critical phases
Waterfall	Sequential project methodology moving through distinct phases

Appendix

Links & Resources

Connect with me

https://linktr.ee/onthepeiroll

Appendix

Podcasts & Articles I've done

[QR]	**Video:** Be More Project Manager with Tom Bassett
[QR]	**Video:** Understanding Power and Politics of Stakeholder Management – Copenhagen Salesforce Architects User Group Oct 2023
[QR]	**Article:** Priming for a Successful Salesforce Project Key things to think about before embarking on a project
[QR]	**Article:** Salesforce Discovery – Ignore these two elements at your peril Two very important things to consider during a Discovery
[QR]	**Article:** Salesforce Discovery – Reap what you SoW why the Statement of Work is important

Additional Resources & Articles

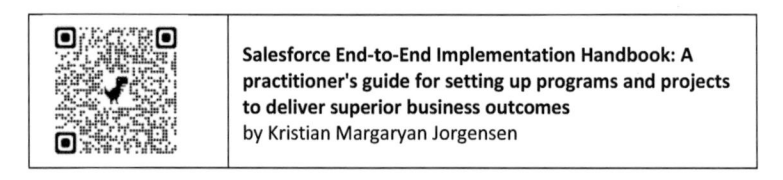

[QR]	Salesforce End-to-End Implementation Handbook: A practitioner's guide for setting up programs and projects to deliver superior business outcomes by Kristian Margaryan Jorgensen

Printed in Dunstable, United Kingdom